A Tryst with Nature

A Tryst with Nature

Labour, Self, and Language

Savyasaachi

Orient BlackSwan

A TRYST WITH NATURE: LABOUR, SELF, AND LANGUAGE

ORIENT BLACKSWAN PRIVATE LIMITED

Registered Office
3-6-752 Himayatnagar, Hyderabad 500 029 (Telangana), INDIA
e-mail: centraloffice@orientblackswan.com

Other Offices
Bengaluru, Chennai, Guwahati, Hyderabad, Kolkata,
Mumbai, New Delhi, Noida, Patna, Visakhapatnam

First published by Orient Blackswan Private Limited 2023

ISBN 978-93-5442-455-7

Typeset in
Dante MT Std 11/13
by Manmohan Kumar, Delhi

037698

Printed in India at
Thomson Press, New Delhi 110 020

Published by
Orient Blackswan Private Limited
3-6-752, Himayatnagar Hyderabad 500 029
e-mail: info@orientblackswan.com

Contents

Tables

Abbreviations

BJA	Bharat Jan Andolan
BPL	below the poverty line
CFI	Community Forestry International
CWLH	critical wildlife habitats
ECOSOC	Economic and Social Council
FPC	Forest Protection Committee
FRA	Forest Rights Act (2006)
GATT	General Agreement on Tariffs and Trade
ICSSR	Indian Council for Social Science Research
ILO	International Labor Organization
IPC	Indian Penal Code
IWGIA	International Work Group for Indigenous Affairs
JFM	Joint Forest Management Programme
KKJS	Koel Karo Jan Sangathan
PCA	Prevention of Cruelty to Animals Act, 1960
PESA	Panchayats Extension to Scheduled Areas Act (1996)
SHGs	self-help groups
TSRDS	Tata Steel Rural Development Society
VSS	Vana Samarakshana Samithi
WTO	World Trade Organization

Glossary

adhe	heat; (sun)light
agarbatti	incense sticks
ako	mother's father
bapi	father's mother
chikla	slush
darm	shade; shadow; cool
dukhi	afflictions
hanal	earthen pot of ancestors
irta	front
kako	mother's mother
kanjkar	dreamtime
kesar gayta	a ritual specialist who uses a knife to sacrifice at the altar of Talurmuttee
leski	ritual specialist
lesna	the state of forgetting (the path taken in the forest); also, the skill of the *leski* in inducing the forgetting of his social being
kaksar	play
mohiria	musician of the Panka clan
nagrche	musicians of the Panka clan, who play the drums
parde	tunes and drum beats
pattari	singer and storyteller, who uses songs, riddles, and stories to describe past social lives
penda	clearing in a forest, intended for cultivation
penu-kaksar	clan festivals, when the relationship between the social being of the Koitors and the specialised skill of a *leski* is discernible as play
poron	back

sat	truth
tado	father's father
tali	short form of Talurmuttee, or mother earth
tori	mud
urvna	elementary healing practice

In Gratitude

This book is a work in progress.

I would like to express gratitude to my teachers, Professor J. P. S. Uberoi and Professor Ashis Nandy. Listening to them, I learnt that studentship is about being wakeful to the 'rhythm' of ideas and respect for all thinking beings—human as well as non-human—in context. This gives vitality to an honest, ethical academic discipline.

Various thoughts in this book have come during *longue duree* hibernations, walks, and cycle rides across forests, villages, towns, and cities. I want to express my gratitude to all the people along these passages who openly shared glimpses of their lives and their predicaments.

Several Koitors of Shringarbhum said to me that thoughts come with the air we breathe, the breeze that touches us, and the winds that flow in and out of our homes. With unconditional generosity and warmth, they showed that to engage with thoughts, one has to be a disciple of the word. In this regard, I express my gratitude to the Koitor people, the *Leski*s (healers) and *pattari*s (epic narrators) of Konge, Sonepur, Garpa, Badapenda, Becha, Kumogubla, and Kongali.

Unconditionality, Ma and Baba showed, is the basis for the mutuality of respect and love. They knew from experience that it brings dignity to thought, work, and social relations. I look up towards the sky to seek their blessings.

My gratitude to Achla, my better half, and son Mohhu for their love and care.

Without the critical warmth of friends, it is difficult to weave a robust relation between thoughts and way of life. For their candour and warmth, I remember affectionately Massiah, Sukhni, Sukmi, Gore, Sukhdei, Sukdas, and Sukamdas from Shringarbhum; Punam,

Smriti, Khalid, and Ritambhara of the Department of Sociology; Madhu the field botanist; the late Smitu Kothari; and the architect, the late Ashish Ganju.

I want to express gratitude to students of the Department of Sociology, Jamia Millia Islamia, who questioned me with curiosity and a commitment to know and understand the world we live in. Their humility is the topsoil for wholesome living. People from Shringarbhum would say that such a student is unique and becomes a *tado*.

I have tried my best to absorb all these learnings in my work. However, all the shortcomings are my responsibility.

Orient BlackSwan's support has been reassuring. I am grateful to Nilanjana Majumdar for her patience and to Proteeti Banerjee for her sharp eye for details and meticulous editing.

Prologue

Learning to Observe

My curiosity to know the horizons of modern social life shaped, to begin with, the fieldwork for my doctoral thesis, which commenced in 1983. It steered me further to look for people whose lives were not shaped by the vocabulary of modern social life, its worldview, and its infrastructure. Where were such people? What was their way of life?

I observed that the pathways opened by this curiosity led to the Koitor forest dwellers in Bastar, to the Kuttia Khonds in Phulbani, and to the Kharias in Mayurbhanj, Odisha. On these pathways, countless conversations, discussions, and debates occurred in a wide variety of locations free from the bindings of clock time, and with a wide diversity of children, young men and women, and elders: forest dwellers, peasants, city dwellers, government officers at all levels, teachers in schools, colleges, and universities in the region and in Delhi, artists, activists, and NGOs. The ethnography and discussion in this book is based on questions, subjects, information, and learnings that emerged from these countless conversations.

Every conversation opened up fields for observing and researching the flows of daily life: its rhythms, its problems, and its existential demands in relation to the kitchen, home, landscapes, public spaces, and institutions.

I observed the inappropriateness of the theory and practice of the 'informant', time-bound interviews, structured questionnaires, thematic focused group discussions, and other similar tools of data collection. These were 'intrusions' into the social life of the people by anthropologists, who are positioned as privileged observers, and who fix people as the passive observed within frames of disciplinary concepts, categories, principles, and methods. All of this rendered the people as 'observed objects', excluding them from the processes of creating knowledge.

On closer scrutiny, it was clear that this observer-centric mode of observation 'othered' the observed. It was legitimised by a history of ideas that privileged the natural sciences over the humanities and social sciences, and was attuned to modes of colonial governance that constructed people as 'objects' to be governed.

This was challenged during the 1960s, when the 'othering' of the 'observed' and the 'governed' was questioned and resisted. This led to a significant shift in social anthropological thinking. With regard to this shift, George W. Stocking, Jr. writes in *Observers Observed*,

> .... special sense of disciplinary crisis that has developed since about 1960. With the withdrawal of the umbrella of European power that long protected their entry into the colonial field, anthropologists found it increasingly difficult to gain access to (as well as ethically more problematic to study) the non-European 'others' who had traditionally excited the anthropological imagination—and who seemed finally about to realize, through cultural change, the long-trumpeted anthropological prediction of the 'vanishing primitive'. (Stocking, Jr. 1983, 4)

This withdrawal occurred on account of the assertions by the 'observed' people across the world to be included in the creation of knowledge and in the modes of governance legitimised by it.

Hereafter, non-European 'others', the 'observed' 'objects' of governance, were in a position to observe researches, their political as well as economic underpinnings, and the dynamics of the postcolonial world. The vanishing primitive patterns of social structure and cultural values, which were different from, and yet parallel to, those that were being introduced by modern industrial development across the world, and which had been studied by classical anthropology before the 1960s, acquired new significance. These became the basis for interrogating, critiquing, and exposing the violence of colonial regimes that were annihilating people and nature.

It opened minds, both inside and outside the university and research institutes, to be attentive to the voices of the 'observed' people as they came forward, denouncing violence, hegemony, and the conquest of peoples and nature, while at the same time emphasising the necessity of learning to listen to nature, which was the basis of their ways of life and worldviews. It became clear that this could make significant contributions to the search for wholesome ways of modern living, different from and radically opposed to the one laid out by observer-centric modes of knowledge and their corresponding systems of governance.

This was an alert for epistemic vigilance to screen out theories and practices that used violent terms, concepts, and categories.

In this context, the anthropologist was no longer the privileged observer, and people and nature were not the passive observed. Both were observers and the observed—the anthropologist was being observed by the people, and by the world of plants and animals as well. This intersubjectivity between the observer and the observed became important, and it bracketed modes of othering 'the observed'.

I observed that this intersubjectivity between the observer and the observed bracketed modes of thinking and doing that othered the observed. That is to say, the constructions of the self, the requirement of institutional norms, and the weight of historical memory inside and outside the university othered this intersubjectivity.

The resistance to othering by social constructions of the self (acquired at home, from peers and institutions) required a mode of unlearning that brackets the taken-for-granted cultural worldview as well as its class, status, and power coordinates. In the absence of this bracketing, the observer-centric position prevails. Consequently, those with higher class status and power cannot be observed, and those lower can be framed for observation. Only when this asymmetry is resisted and dissolved can the equality, fraternity, and liberty between observer and observed be nurtured.

Here, nurturing is a way of resisting. Learning the language of the people by letting go of the informant is one way to resist the othering of the 'observed' and of nurturing the intersubjectivity. I witnessed a strong opposition to this from institutions.

An instance will illustrate this. My first progress report to the Indian Council for Social Science Research (ICSSR) was a list of words I had learnt from the Koitors. This was considered inadequate as well as inappropriate, and my doctoral scholarship was annulled.

Several people within and outside the university read this as a delegitimisation of my studentship. I was told my research was against the grain of historical memory that held that forest dwellers were the past of modern societies. I was discouraged with the warning that my work represented a backward movement in time, away from the expanding horizons of modern sciences, technologies, and social life. I was told that learning the language of Koitors was not necessary. This delegitimisation, I observed, upheld an observer-centric mode of extracting 'clock time' from people's daily routine for filling in data sheets.

I did try to work with informants. Soon, I realised that this reduced me to a dumb spectator who understood nothing of the informants' conversation with the people. This deprived me of interaction with the people, pulled people out from their everyday activity, froze the passage of time, and privileged the informants over people in the community. I thus took a decision to let go of the informant.

Hereafter, people walked in and out of conversations, uninhibited. I learnt to listen and see, letting go of the observer-centric mode of research. Every moment contributed to tuning in to rhythms of fading in and out of social life. In all conversations, glimpses of autobiography were shared. This was a cordial way to become familiar with the unfamiliar. Thus there were very few direct questions asked of me: what was my name, where did I come from, and what did I do. My response was simple: I told them my name, said I was a student, and that I had come to learn the language of the people.

The 'field was unfolding at its own pace, it was guiding fieldwork', as it were. In this situation, there was no time or place for conventional research methods. The use of questionnaires, conducting interviews, organising focus group discussions would have undermined the intersubjectivity between the observer and the observed.

Over time, I was 'invisibly present' in all situations. I was 'present', but my presence did not interfere with the occurrences of social life. The rhythms and pace of fieldwork were coeval with the unfolding, neither faster nor slower. There was a reciprocity between the observer and the observed in this mode of being present in the field.

I observed an inbuilt reflexivity that ensured mutual respect for social and cultural boundaries. I was observing myself as an observer, with the awareness that all people of the community often discussed me, comparing notes. These conversations were sometimes shared with me. It was not necessary for me to know more. Its significance was that it cleared the ground for listening to everyone without being opinionated.

I observed that being non-opinionated has three aspects. *First*, it allowed for seamless (uninhibited) expression of admissible and inadmissible opinions, and unmentionable views, positions, emotions, discomforts, likes, dislikes, idiosyncrasies on the one hand, and unlimited open-ended cordial discussions, criticism, and disagreement, on the other. *Second*, it required respecting the trust generated in the course of sharing and holding in confidence what was shared. Thus, anyone could listen in. This built trust by way of restraining both partners in the intersubjectivity, from the uncritical acceptance of claims, propositions, conclusions, definitions. *Third*, it created a community that encouraged self-correction. This included the observer and the observed as equal partners in the creation of knowledge. This interdependence generated rhythms of learning and diverse expositions of the passage of time. Such intersubjectivity encouraged active epistemic vigilance to shelter the observer and the observed from being 'othered' by observer-centric modes.

It freed the observer from the restlessness, sterile and morbid objectivity which framed the observed in the observer's exposition of time and not their own. I observed that this morbidity deprived the observed of the language to which it belongs and undermined the observer's capacity to express and observe its-self. Such objectivist epistemic agency distorts perception because it pays no heed to the significance of difference in the passage of time between the observer and the observed: either the observer is moving several times faster than the observed or the observed is moving several times faster than the observer. On account of this difference, objectivist agency is overtaken by anxiety and by the fetish of empirical evidence.

From the objectivist standpoint, the forest horizon is one of physical resources and no more. The horizon as seen from the partnership of the observer and the observed is different, and contrary to the one generated by the observer-centric position. On account of this partnership, the universe of the forest is intelligible as a horizon of a social living space, inclusive of interconnecting habitats of living and non-living beings. Its wholeness has a presence with no equivalence, and it resists the observer-centric worldview. There are three elements in each horizon, namely labour, language, and self. The difference between these two notions of horizon are discussed in seven chapters of the book.

Chapter One focuses on the difference between horizons of reflexive labor and instrumental labour. Chapter Two provides the ethnography of the Koitors' language of self and reflexive labor, which holds together living and non-living beings in the universe of the forest. Koitors are located in north Bastar, Chhattisgarh. Chapter Three draws attention to the way the language of two legislations—the Panchayats Extension to Scheduled Areas Act (PESA, 1996) and the Forest Rights Act (FRA, 2006)—marginalised reflexive labor. Chapter Four discusses the language of instrumental labour underlying these legislations.. Chapter Five highlights the difference between caretakers' reflexivity and conquerors' instrumentalism. Chapter Six underlines the hermeneutic injustice consequent to the denial of one's own language in order to uphold value generated either from utility or from scarcity, or from the objectification of subjectivity. Chapter Seven discusses the significance of language, labor, and self for generating and conserving the topsoil of modern social life.

one

Elements of Nature

Abstract and Concrete*

Since the very beginning of discussions on the environment and ecological crisis, the term 'nature' has been used to refer to atoms, molecules, physical laws on the one hand, as well as to living beings such as dogs, tigers, birds, elephants, etc., and to natural landscapes. I would like to suggest that these two sets of elements are neither the same nor similar. The first set is an abstraction and a part of culture, insofar as labour is necessary for the making of an oxygen molecule, and the second set is a part of the concrete natural world, which is an expression of labor, and has received no contribution of human labour in its making. This difference is important.

In this chapter, I will try to argue that there is a difference between H2O and water. The former is abstract, the latter is concrete. These look alike, but metabolise differently and are the basis of the difference between horizons of reflexive labor and instrumental labour.

'*A Posteriori* Identity' of H2O and the Instrumental Labour

David Barnett points out that Saul Kripke (1980 [1972]) has argued that, '... proper names rigidly designate their referents, that empirical

*A large part of this chapter has been taken from my article, 'Water and H2O: Elements of Labo(u)r', published in *The Economic and Political Weekly* 54 (37), 14 September 2019.

investigation is sometimes needed to establish co reference, and therefore ... there are certain identities which are necessary a posteriori' (2000, 101).

Barnett formulates the *a posteriori* identity for H2O as follows: 'If "H2O" and "water" do in fact rigidly designate the same stuff, then, necessarily, water is identical to H2O' (Barnett 2000, 101). This has a history. David P. Miller (2004, 1) points out that Joseph Priestley and Henry Cavendish, scientists of the eighteenth century, discovered that water, a compound (H2O), is made up of smaller elements (oxygen and hydrogen), and that this was a refutation of the Greek view that water was a primordial element. This had been regarded as commonsense, respected by ancient people and discussed by early Greek philosophers.

This refutation made it a posteriori identity and rendered commonsense dysfunctional. According to Hasok Chang (2012, 14), when Priestley and Cavendish declared that water was a compound of elements, they 'clearly meant element to be a substance that could be modified, by the addition or subtraction of phlogiston'. He asks,

> What was phlogiston? In short, it was the principle of inflammability; 'principle' here did not mean a fundamental rule, but rather a fundamental substance that combined with other substances and gave them its characteristic properties. Phlogiston was the principle that imparted combustibility to combustibles. A combustible substance was rich in phlogiston, and when it burned it released its phlogiston, which then manifested itself in the flame that came out. (ibid., 3)

Chang further points out,

> No one knew better than Priestley how to make oxygen (dephlogisticated air), and hydrogen (called inflammable air) that had been discovered and studied in 1766 by his compatriot and fellow phlogistonist Henry Cavendish.
>
> The ... Cavendish–Priestley view was that inflammable air was 'phlogisticated water', that is, water containing an excess of phlogiston. As for oxygen, or dephlogisticated air, that was 'dephlogisticated water'. When phlogisticated water and dephlogisticated water combined with each other, the excess and deficit of phlogiston cancelled out and plain water was produced. (ibid., 6)

This *a posteriori* property of H2O to impart 'combustibility to combustibles' is a fundamental of the metabolic exchange between man and nature initiated by labour. The time and energy expended to make H2O is the phlogiston of labour. That is to say, labour is the capacity for combustion, to impart combustibility to combustibles. As a rule, this separates and combines natural substances. From the very beginning, this has shaped the character of the industrial labour system.

For this reason, it will be appropriate to conceptualise H2O as a part of the stuff of industrial labour, a means to convert the use value of this discovery into commodities with exchange value. This is the metabolism of homogenisation. It produces what Jean Paul Sartre describes as 'inert totalities'. One such product is the homogenised 'a posteriori identity' of H2O. The notion of 'inert totality' given by Sartre has four attributes.

> A totality is defined as a being which, while radically distinct from the sum of its parts, is present in its entirety, in one form or another, in each of these parts, and which relates to itself either through its relation to one or more of its parts or through its relation to the relations between all or some of them.
>
> If this reality is created (a painting or a symphony are examples ...), it can exist only in the imaginary (l'imaginaire), ... as the correlative of an act of imagination.
>
> The ontological status to which it lays claim by its very definition is that of the in-itself, the inert. The synthetic unity produced its appearance of not an activity, but only the vestige of a past action.
>
> Through its being-in-exteriority, the inert in-itself gnaws away at this appearance of unity; the passive totality is, in fact, eroded infinite divisibility. (Sartre 2004, 45)

Each of these four attributes is discernible in H2O. As a totality, H2O is 'radically distinct from the sum of its parts' (hydrogen and oxygen), and 'it is present in its entirety, in one form or another, in each of these parts, and which relates to itself either through its relation to one or more of its parts or through its relation to the relations between all or some of them' (ibid.). That is to say, it is related to nothing outside of itself.

This makes a posteriori identity, H2O, exist as an imaginary (l'imaginaire), as the correlative of an act of imagination. Nowhere outside this imagination can H2O be found to exist. As a homogenous abstraction, it is 'in-itself' inert. This is because the synthetic unity of hydrogen and oxygen molecules produced its appearance (water) as a 'vestige of past actions' of substance modification by separation and combination, and not as an organic activity.

The appearance of abstract H2O exists as 'being-in-exteriority'. Its passive totality is eroded by its infinite divisibility (to become a substance that could be modified, by addition or subtraction). The notion of infinite divisibility represents a scientific consciousness in all sciences. Its watchword is 'empirical facts', which are opposed to abstract cultural concepts. This, Luce Irigaray says, is '… To designate one part of matter—as theme, motif, referent, method—while neglecting the whole of its domain …' (1999, 11–12). Here, Irigaray argues that the logic of the matter of *physis*[1] is not known to *logos* (ibid., 11).

The most damaging consequence of the infinitely divisible is the disturbance of the wholesomeness of longer inclusive water-cycles, the dehydration of riverbeds, and depletion of groundwater and fresh-water reserves.

WATER AND REFLEXIVE LABOR

Questioning a posteriori identity of H2O, Barnett asks,

> Is the possibility of there being a sample of H2O that is not a sample of water merely one of epistemic nature? The answer is no.
>
> …
>
> This intuition is driven not by the empirical fact that water is composed of H2O, but rather by an a priori fact about water. (2000, 107)

What could this *a priori* fact be, other than its primordiality as the root of all things! To the water of Thales, the air of Anaximenes, and the fire of Heraclitus, he (Empedocles) adds earth, and declares them as all alike: primeval, the promise and the potency, 'The fourfold root of all things' (Leonard 1908, 5). Timothy Crowley points out that,

> The view that fire, air, water, and earth are the constituents of things appears to be something of a commonplace by Plato's time .... these four 'Empedoclean' elements were commonly or popularly called archai and stoicheia of everything by Plato's contemporaries .... The meaning of archai is 'the original sources or principles of things'; and of stoicheia, 'the ultimate constituents of things'. (Crowley 2005, 380)
>
> ... Three usages of stoicheion ... Aristotle explicitly identifies are ... the 'alphabetic' sense, the second the 'elemental' sense, and the third, referring as it does to the principles, axioms, and postulates of geometry, the 'geometric' sense. (ibid., 374)
>
> It is important to emphasize that these three senses ... are independent of each other, and hence that each can be understood without reference to the other. (ibid., 375)

Crowley further points out that Plato compares fire, air, water, and earth with syllables. This, Crowley argues, is because Plato

> ... believes that fire, air, water, and earth are not the ultimate constituents of things, and to make this point clearly and sharply, he denies that they are even as basic as *syllabai*. (2005, 381)
>
> There is an allusion to the alphabetic sense of *stoicheion*. Perhaps it should be noted that the reference to *syllabe* is not necessarily a reference to alphabetic syllables: just as *stoicheion* has a core meaning of 'primary constituent', so it is sometimes suggested that *syllabe* has a basic or primitive sense of 'that which is held together'—that is, of several things held together; hence a composite or complex, as opposed to a simple, object. (ibid., 382; emphasis in the original)

Water is one such element. Its primordiality is a complex phenomenon: it is a syllable and its physis is understood as that which is held together—that is, several things held together. This makes it the root of all things.

To grasp this, I follow a fundament of Goethe's method to observe common phenomenon outside the laboratory. In landscapes, water occurs in heterogeneous terrains and its movements metabolise the planet earth. In this all-pervasiveness, its primordial *a priori*-ness is discernible. With *entelechy*, can we see that H2O is mere matter and water is a living body? 'Entelechy is that which makes the difference between mere matter and a living body.'[2]

The syllabe water is a living body as it hydrates, holds together the Sensible form of a living body, and brings colour to all living beings. Each of these aspects of life is elaborated here. Goethe discovered the Sensible form in his study of plants.

J. P. S. Uberoi points out that it is the *Urphaenomen* or the archetype. Archetypes or Urphaenomen, is defined by Goethe as the 'entelechy of a series of sensible structural forms. It is self-existent or self-sustaining and self-explanatory unity of the real and the ideal, the precept and the concept' (1984, 26). The primordial identity of water is the Urphaenomen. It hydrates and holds together. It is the element which is present above, on, and below the surface of earth to hold together all living beings in these three realms. Its fluidity is a series of sensible forms (liquid, vapour, and solid) which hold together other sensible forms in the sky, on the earth, and underground. There is a self-explanatory unity of the real and the ideal, the precept and the concept in its fluidity and transparency.

Goethe describes this physis[3] of the Urphaenomen in the discussion on Metamorphosis. In Goethe's words,

> It is like [a] centrifugal force and would lose itself in the infinite if a counter-weight were not provided. I am referring to [b] the specification force, that tenacious capacity for persistence inherent in whatever has attained existence, a centripetal force that cannot be disturbed in its deepest nature by anything external. (Goethe, quoted in Uberoi 1984, 30)

This counterweight is discernible.

> True observers of nature ... will agree that all which presents itself in appearance, all that we meet with as phenomena, must either indicate its original division which is capable of union, or an original unity which admits of division and, that the phenomenon will present itself accordingly. To divide the united, to unite the divided, is the life of nature; this is the eternal systole and diastole, the eternal collapsion

> and expansion, the inspiration and expiration of the world in which we live and move. (ibid., 31)

The 'centrifugal force that would lose itself in the infinite if a counter-weight were not provided' is discernible as water changes, as it transforms from solid to liquid to vapour.

Here, we meet with water as a primordial phenomenon, which indicates its original division which is capable of union, and an original unity which admits of division. The sensible form of water functions to divide the united, to unite the divided.

As regards bringing colour to living beings, it is colourlessness that makes the holding together all-inclusive. Does colourless water not bring colour to this biodiversity? Are not the colours of the rainbow in the sky taken by colourless water to the biodiversity of plants, birds, and animals on earth? What 'is' the water that does this? This is not known to the logos of the 'empirical fact H2O'.

Small quantities of fresh water appear colourless. However, in open spaces fresh water has a slight blue colour, which becomes deeper as the thickness of the observed sample increases. This blue hue shows an intrinsic property of water, namely the scattering and selective absorption (polarisation and progression)[4] of white light. However, when we observe a rainbow, we notice that water reflects, scatters, and absorbs all the colours of white light. These absorbed colours are carried to all sensible forms of the life-world.

For instance, only leaves hydrate and enable the selective absorption of colours that occur in the white sunlight that falls on it. I wonder if Goethe would consider this another reason as to why a plant is all leaf.

With regard to plants, Henri Bortoft wrote,

> Hypothesis: All is leaf. This simplicity makes possible all diversity. The leaf he refers to here is to be understood in the universal sense as an omnipotent form and not as a particular leaf. The different organs of the plant are then perceived as the metamorphic variation of this form, each of which could be derived from any of the others. This is continuity of form and not of substance. (1996, 80)

The differentiation of plants into diversity by this entelechy is the metamorphosis.

No hydrated plant in full blossom looks like any other, and yet all of them appear as one unified whole. It is because of the presence of water that the unity of different sensible plant forms is discernible in their self-activity. Each plant, and all plants, are self-existent or self-sustaining and self-explanatory. The entelechy that is discernible in their self-activity shows that each unique plant has a resemblance to all other equally unique plants.

On Labo(u)r and Conservation—Some Reflections

There is a fundamental difference between water represented minimally as a chemical compound H2O and landscape water that pours from the sky, flows in the rivers, and merges with the ocean. Both look alike. The similar appearance draws attention to the fact that both are necessary and essential for the making of the societal labour metabolism nexus. The subtle difference is intelligible in the way these metabolise labo(u)r differently. The different spellings 'labour' and 'labor' refer to its instrumental and reflexive aspects, respectively.

The former (H2O) is composed of concrete abstract elements and the latter, known since the very beginning of creation, is a concrete element of natural landscapes. The long history of the discussion on the meaning of abstract and concrete has been described by Evald Ilyenkov (2013 [1960], Chs 1 and 2). For our discussion, it will suffice to know that,

> The concrete is here a full synonym of the sensually perceived, individual, carnal, mundane, transient ('composite and therefore doomed to disintegration, to disappearance). The abstract is a synonym of the eternal, imperishable, indivisible, divinely instituted, universal, absolute, etc. (Ilyenkov 2013 [1960], 14)

This makes landscape water concrete. Its being there since time immemorial makes it primordial.

In the sixteenth and seventeenth centuries, with the use of natural sciences for manufacturing, a labour process experimentally isolated things, abstracted from them the content properties, relations, and states of things, and represented these with names as independent things. This was use value. To this was added more labour to make goods and services worthy of exchange. These are concrete abstractions.

Here,

> 'Concreteness' is neither a synonym for nor a privilege of the sensual-image form of reflection of reality in consciousness, just as 'abstractness' is not a specific characteristic of rational theoretical knowledge. Certainly we speak, as often as not, of the concreteness of a sensual image and of abstract thought. (Ilyenkov 2013 [1960], 37)

The chemistry of the abstract concreteness of H2O metabolises[5] instrumental labour to distance, separate, and free man from the natural environment. This distancing, Georg Lukacs (1980 [1978], 25–28), argues, is the model for all social practices. This reinforces a societal labour metabolism nexus,[6] which is the cause of dehydration. When H2O directs and metabolises labor, its physis[7] dehydrates.

Landscape water is concrete primordial, and it metabolises reflexive labor that orients human beings to discover their potentiality from what they do and can do to maintain the coeval-ness and the seamless continuum with their natural environment, and not be distanced and separate from it. Thus, they see their reflection in the enrichment of the diversity of all living beings. The reflexivity of this labor is grounded in a wholistic science, which considers non-human living beings as well as natural phenomena as equal (and not as antagonistic) contributors in the making of life, society, and culture. When primordial water directs and metabolises labor, its physis, that is, its self-active reflexivity—an inner necessity—holds it together, and with this it hydrates and holds together all living beings.

The prominence of concrete primordial landscape water is discernible from the blue-coloured image of earth when seen from outer space. This distinguishes it from other planets in the cosmos. This prominence is derived from the fact that 75 per cent of landscape is water, and 60 per cent to 100 per cent of the bodies of living beings is water.

This image does not show that most of the 75 per cent water distributed over landscapes is poisoned; it is not colourless, not odourless, and not sweet to taste. It is black in colour, it stinks, and it will have a nasty taste, if at all someone were to try tasting it.

This difference draws attention to the 'want' for fresh water from diverse sources—groundwater, fresh-water lakes, and springs—for hydrating living beings. For it is fresh 'natural water' which holds the landscape together. It is fluid, transparent, and colourless, which makes it odourless or gives it a pleasant smell, makes it tasteless as well as sweet to taste, depending on time and place. Its transparent 'self-activity' makes it 'self-existent or self-sustaining'. It is each of these attributes that holds together the series of sensible forms that make up a landscape.

The Rights regimes of conservation have moved on from animal rights[8] to the rights of mother earth,[9] and now to rights of habitat.[10] However, these do not stand on firm ground so long as the necessity for fresh landscape water is not included as the foundation of conservation.

These Rights regimes are post-destruction dispensations that perpetuate the orientation of instrumental labour to not give adequate and appropriate recognition to the fact that landscape water, and not H2O, is primordial for the metabolism of everything on planet earth. This is demonstrated by the fact that conservation of water and conservation of biodiversity take place on two different registers.

These regimes are helpless when flood waters destroy human habitations. Further, they are powerless to ensure that rivers continue to flow seamlessly so that all living beings can get water. Furthermore, these regimes cannot protect 'conservation sites' from the excess carbon released by modern economies in the neighbourhood. There is a limit to the absorption of carbon; if this limit is transgressed, then the metabolism of these habitats changes.

These regimes are oriented to protect human beings and natural biodiversity habitats from each other.

With a shift to reflexive labor, it will be possible to firmly ground conservation in the primordiality of water. This would bring the conservation of water and the conservation of biodiversity on one register; make one habitat for human beings alongside natural biodiversity; and restrain the production of carbon.

Most significantly, with this shift from a posteriori identity of H2O to water, understood as the unchanging material principle of life, it will be possible to see conservation become a habit in everyday life. This will begin to hydrate, hold together, and bring colour to all living beings. Of special significance is colour, because it is the expression of the light that illuminates life.

Endnotes

1. In pre-Socratic Greek culture, there were four divisions of cosmology. 'To each of these four divisions—primal matter, form, the efficient causal agent, and God the final cause, the one-word *physis* may be applied. If we take a pantheistic view, and regard the four divisions as limitations in the way of regarding the pantheos, we may call the whole *physis*' (Knowlton 1920, 226).

2. *Entelechy* is a philosophical concept stemming from Aristotle's metaphysics, and generally used to identify whatever it is that makes the difference between mere matter and a living body. Originally a notion merely concerning the actualisation of the potential of some substance (and so a notion that easily fits into a naturalistic description of the world), in Leibniz's hands it came to denote a non-material, unextended, mind-like entity that underlies the entire physical world. In each case, the driving thought is that something metaphysically distinctive must be present in living bodies. See https://www.newworldencyclopedia.org/entry/Entelechy (accessed March 2023).

3. 'Physis is nearest to natural science which deals with problems that at the present day concern physics, chemistry, and biology, and which has the attitude of studying cause and effect, as distinguished from purpose' (Knowlton 1920, 241).

4. From his study of Goethe, Uberoi 'derives the comprehensive formula that, in the study of man and nature, polarity + progression = dialectics, always remembering of course that there will be also the inverse shadow dialectics of separation and regression' (Uberoi 1984, 65).

5. It captures the complex biochemical process of metabolic exchange, through which an organism (or a given cell) draws upon materials and

energy from its environment and converts these by way of various metabolic reactions into the building blocks of growth. In addition, the concept of metabolism is used to refer to the specific regulatory processes that govern this complex interchange between organisms and their environment. Eugene Odum and other leading system ecologists now employ 'metabolism' to refer to all biological levels, starting with the single cell and ending with the ecosystem. See Foster (2000, 160).

6. This nexus is a complex of interconnections between the laboratory perception of nature, which dis-embeds and dislocates the economy of nature from society.

7. The concept of *physis* comes to us from ancient Greek culture. According to Edgar C. Knowlton (1920, 224–225), it arose long before its actual personification in literature or theological deifications under the specific name. It was gradually defined by pre-Socratic philosophers.

8. For instance, it is illegal to give injurious substances to animals; to transport animals in a manner that will cause them harm or suffering (PCA, Section 11); to maim or cause them injury for monetary value (IPC, Sections 428 and 429).

9. The Universal Declaration of the Rights of Mother Earth, 22 April 2010.

10. Baigas have been given habitat rights. See Narayanan (2015) and Chakravarty (2016).

two

Reflexive Labor[1]

Koitors and the Universe of the forest

Koitor labor is reflexive. Koitors are located in north Bastar, Chhattisgarh. This chapter provides an ethnography of the Koitors' language of self and reflexive labor, which holds together living and non-living beings in the universe of the forest. It is best expressed in the phrase, 'the belongings of a person should not be more than the person can carry'.

The unceasing repetition of cultivation cycles that shift from one plot to the other over twenty-four such plots unfolds to the Koitors different aspects of the universe of the forest. It is a living space in a double sense: *first*, it is itself alive, vibrant, and animated; *second*, it animates the social existence of everything living and non-living.

This view of the universe of the forest landscape cannot be understood if the forest is regarded as a resource or an endowment or a provider of services. For the Koitor, the instrumental value of the forest is framed by Kanjkar or dream-time; for, like dreams, the forest dissolves and regenerates itself. This is a privileged time for the Koitors, because they derive from it all the knowledge necessary to earn a livelihood and live in the forest.

The phenomenon of natural regeneration of the forest landscape provides an abundance of forest produce that, on the one hand, supplements the produce from cultivation, and on the other, induces *lesna*, a state of forgetting, as the return of the forest veils the horizon. For example, when the Koitors are unable to return home after either hunting or gathering food or collecting sacred herbal plants in the forests, in their mind the forest gets transmuted into a metaphor which enables an understanding of a particular relation between memory and forgetting.

Since the phenomenon of the return of the forest on *penda*, or plots cleared for cultivation, is related by association to the 'historic act' of cutting trees, it can be concluded that this return is concomitant with that 'historic act'. In the case of cultivation, the 'historic act' of cutting trees patterns memory and forgetting along the cultivation cycle. The function of the latter is not to devalue the 'historic act'; on the contrary, it draws attention to a process of dissolution and to the relation between elements of nature, both of which give meaning to the 'historic act' itself and to its memory.

The Koitors view nature as open and raw, as it were, framed by and framing the *penda* cultivation cycle. It is neither fragmented nor atomised under the lens of a laboratory microscope. The forest can thus be viewed from two positions: from that of the Koitors who live in it and earn their livelihood as landless people—because they are only caretakers on behalf of Talurmuttee, the old mother earth—and from the position of the outsiders, viz., the plains people, who use it only as a resource. The differences between the two positions are brought out sharply in the way trees are cut.

In penda cultivation, trees are so cut as to allow for their regeneration to veil the horizon. In contrast, for the plains people, trees are cut to prepare rice fields or raise a plantation, whereby the horizon is open to sight and the multiplicity of forest life is lost irretrievably. The forest is sacred for the Koitors, who move between these two worlds—that of the plains and that of the forest. The ideas of forest as sacred grove belong to their tradition. But the ideas of forest as resource belong to the rational scientific colonial tradition. The former is understood on the basis of the analogy of the self-activity of the forest, and the latter is understood as a process of dissolution of the culture of the Koitors. From a position inside the forest landscape, the work of landscape nature dissolves the work of man; and from a position outside the forest on the plains, the work of man dissolves the work of landscape nature.

The Koitors' skill of shifting penda cultivation is grounded in an understanding that its critical limits are co-extensive with the capacity of the forest landscape for self-regeneration, on account of which the presence of the forest landscapes is internal to, and is a necessary condition for, the cultivation process. There is a collateral relation between the economy of nature and the nature of economy. That is to say, the production and reproduction in landscape nature is the norm for the production and reproduction in shifting cultivation.

In their cultivation practice, they maintain a temporal continuum between the work of man and the work of nature, which is differentiated into the following three contiguous periods common to several varieties of shifting cultivation practices. The *first* begins with clearing a forest site and ends with harvest. In this period, the soil regenerative capacity is harnessed. The *second* comprises long fallow periods, to rest the earth and stem the growing loss of fertility on account of cropping and erosion. *Third* is a period of regeneration of the forest landscape during which the soil is prepared again for cultivation.

Thus, a clearing on the forest landscape changes its appearance from a penda plot to a forest gradually as the clearing dissolves on account of the self-activity of landscape nature. Accordingly, the significance of longer years of fallow in impermanent clearings of short duration is that it allows a long period for forest regeneration. This accounts for temporal continuity, which renders the presence of the forests immanent to the Koitors' way of life. The Koitors perceive its empirical aspects in the self-regeneration of the flora and fauna in the forest in all their multiplicity and abundance, and its ideal aspect in the dissolution of a penda. The self-activity of nature expresses the unity of the empirical and the ideal. A process of making clearings in the forest by cutting trees and the symmetrical dissolution of clearings into forest on account of forest regeneration together constitute the phenomenal universe of their living space. In the former, a forest is home, a place and condition of work, and in the latter, it is an animated universe, mobile and alive.

Primordial Forest Landscape

Shringarbhum is a forest landscape that brings with it a sense of everlasting life. This is represented in the cult of Talurmuttee, mother-goddess earth, associated with the primordial forest landscapes where cultivation is taboo. Often, only medicine-men, that is, *leski*, who know of sacred plants and roots and herbs, can enter here. With their knowledge of these plants they cure the sick and send them back to work. In all Koitor settlements, this primordial forest is associated with the *nate* (village settlement) Talurmuttee. Other Talurmuttee are associated with places of work, or *buti*. Different *kesar gayta* (a ritual specialist who uses a knife for sacrifice at the altar of Talurmuttee) are caretakers of these *tali*.

In terms of natural phenomena, the forest regenerates itself through its own spontaneous self-activity. The Koitors and other forest dwellers know this from their detailed knowledge of different lifecycles, from birth to dissolution, of plants and animals. The repetition of these cycles takes place over different durations of time, ranging between the annual regeneration or self-reproduction of weeds, of the wild fruits and flowers which form the objects of food-gathering by women, and the approximately 100-year cycles of bamboo, which flower and produce milk before they dissolve and regenerate. The knowledge of several cycles of varying duration associated with the variety and abundance of plant and animal life conjures up the forest landscape universe as a camouflage, whose certainty is founded on the self-activity of nature. In this understanding of the phenomenal universe of a forest, the idea of the self-reproduction of the same plants and animals is underscored by notions of timelessness, regeneration, and everlasting life.

In contrast, the life-span of the human forest dwellers is limited in its time duration of self-reproduction to a generation. A person will definitely witness the death of a relative, friend, or foe within their own lifetime. However, only some persons of some distant generation have been, or will be, witness to the dissolution and regeneration of the bamboo forest. This temporal contrast between humans and nature is significant for an understanding of some aspects of the Koitors' social life, and structures an idea of shared common lands and its relation to the rights of use of persons. The forest landscape is regarded as the work of nature, and therefore cannot be an object of possession and ownership. Only those who recognise the differences between its variety of life forms can acquire rights of possession—but not of ownership, because the Koitor believes that one cannot own that which is not the result of one's own work. The rights to use land can only be transferred collectively by transferring the rights to propitiate Talurmuttee.

A temporary enclosure around the fields defines time-bound rights over the crops raised by the work of men and women. In shifting cultivation, these temporary rights over penda are dissolved through the dissolution of the land into the forest. During cultivation, the work of men and women in the fields contrasts with the work of nature in the forest. Here, the forest is the commons, to be shared for food-gathering and hunting. This is in contrast to the exclusive rights to crops cultivated in penda. The alternation between the work of nature and the work of humans structures a penda cultivation cycle. This is also an alternation between a cleared field and a forest.

Reading the Forest

Koitors depend on the timeliness of summer and monsoon for a healthy harvest. Scientists know the time for rainfall from the data of past seasons. The more the data recorded, the easier it is to follow the monsoon trend.

In contrast, Koitors read the timeliness from the changes in the lifecycles of different living beings inhabiting the forest. The knowledge of annual regeneration cycles is used by the Koitors to mark the time for structuring cultivation work. The time that *kehlapurks* (centipedes) regenerate is the time that weeding operations are undertaken. This is similar to the way the forest is read by forest-dwellers. Ramnath (1988) points out, for instance, that with the onset of the monsoons, many plants, such as the *Kodama*, begin to flower. Black ants appear in long, winding rows from cracks in the ground. Some birds, like the *Goborliti*, migrate away from the forest, as they do every year when summer draws to a close. Koitors rely on these indicators to read changes in the weather and to apprehend the passing of time. Their memory and their ability to read such signs is part of their tradition of cultivation. Irregularity of monsoons, according to Koitors, can be known from deviations in plant and animal lifecycles. The following are a few examples.

Mushrooms, which usually appear during the wet season, do so in a specific order. An understanding of this order makes it easy to tell which stage of the monsoon is in progress. The *manai* mushroom, which normally appears at the end of summer, was seen in the first few days of September in an unusual year.

The *Thummi* plant, which has a root like that of turmeric, flowers every year when the rainy season begins. After the monsoon when the leaves shrivel and fall, the wild boars dig up the thick root to eat. But in that year the boars did not wait for the leaves of Thummi to dry; they dug up the roots well before the rains ended.

Kenoil (red ants), which are eaten by both humans and bears, often build their nests in the folds of green leaves on very tall trees. Normally egg-laying stops when summer ends; but with an erratic monsoon, nests containing eggs and young ones continued to be found even in August. The bird Goborliti disappears from these forests when the summer begins, and it returns when the monsoon is over.

With the help of these readings of the forest, the cultivators are able to maintain a correspondence between the natural cycle and the cultivation cycle. The self-regeneration of nature is common to both. In the alternation between a clearing and the forest in a penda, the work of nature dissolves the work of man. This process is initiated by the use of an axe, and explains some aspects of memory and forgetting in the social history of the Koitor. Each time clearings are made and the forest regenerates, the Koitors recreate the historic act of cutting trees to settle and cultivate the land.

The Forest as Home, Place, and Condition of Work

The forest is internalised by the Koitors, who remain in a continuous relation with it. This is the Koitors' individuation. The Koitors believe that before birth, a child is influenced by its mother's desires and feelings, and also by *darm* (shades) in a forest landscape. A fair child, *pandral*, indicates the influence of darm of the spirit *rau*. A dark child, *kariyal*, is considered normal. The desire of a pregnant mother for certain kinds of food and drink are given priority; these are understood by the Koitors to be those of the child itself. All efforts are made to fulfil the child's desires. This is an extraordinary convention; for, in ordinary circumstances, a woman in a household is usually the last person to eat.

A child is born in the open forest landscape, not within the four walls of a house. The Koitor women believe that several unknown factors may prevent their labour. In their minds, the idea of conception is expressed by the term *peeshkan*, a question: Who will live? The term suggests the possibility that at the time of birth, either both the mother and child, or only one of them, will survive.

The idea of conception and birth denotes three movements: (*i*) a movement from the internal environment into the external environment; (*ii*) this movement is attended by apprehensions of death; (*iii*) it internalises the influences of darm and initiates the child into the universe of the forest as a part of her/his social environment.

While the child is suckling, it is carried during the day astride the mother's hips, tied to her with a large cloth. This facilitates the demand-feeding and, at the same time, familiarises the child with the forest landscape. According to the Koitors, the transmission of warmth at the time of suckling is simultaneous with the transformation of the mother's milk into blood in a child's body. This unity of mother and child goes together with the separation of wife from husband, a convention which is based on the Koitors' belief that if a man sleeps with his wife while the child is suckling, the milk will be transformed into blood within the body of the mother. Consequently, the child would not receive nourishment and its growth would be stunted.

At night, when asleep, the child rests in a basket hung above the ground next to the fire. A child's father and other male members of a household clear the forest to cultivate food crops, to get wood for fire, to keep the hearth alive, and to construct a house. It is believed that to a child, the heat and shelter emanating from wood are signs of both the presence of the forest and of his father and other male members of the household.

When the child is weaned from its mother, s/he is assigned a place to sleep on the ground between the parents. This movement from the basket to the ground opens up a new universe for exploration. The child meets other children, crawls and touches the ground, sees things, plays with mud, pieces of wood, and leaves, and also encounters dogs, cats, and chickens, and begins to learn about its environment. The child playfully manipulates these elements of the forest and of social life as material, in the image of the social activities of elders, of which s/he is a silent observer. For example, children make a hut which is a replica of their parents' hut. Boys hunt, girls cook meals, and they imitate the conversation of elders.

When a child learns to walk, gender differences are given social recognition. The child is given a seamless piece of cloth to wear around the loins. This marks both gender differences and her/his membership to a work group. The male child accompanies the father and the female accompanies the mother.

A child has to learn to live in such a manner that its belongings do not weigh more than what can be carried. This is necessary to become an adult working member of a household. A boy wears a loin cloth the length of four to five arms. He carries an axle on his shoulder, a knife, and a tobacco pouch around his waist. The girl wears a *lugga*—an unstitched piece of cloth about seven arms in length and two arms in width. She wraps it around her waist at one end and takes it over her breasts at the other. During work, the body is minimally clad, and contact between the bare body and the forest is direct and unmediated.

The Bare Body and the Forest Landscape

The bare body is crucial to individuation since the near absence of clothes brings the body in direct relation to the forest. It is the observer, the observed, and the medium of observation. The presence of the forest is absorbed along all contours of the Koitor's body. The body is enveloped by the forest and all dimensions of the forest are measured by the body. Equally, changes in the forest through seasons influence work habits, shape the body, and determine the colour and texture of the skin. They also determine the tactility of the senses, their capacity for endurance, and the acquisition of work skills.

For the Koitors, as for other forest dwellers in tropical climates, clothes perhaps had their origin not as a means of protection against weather, but as a part of the human search for adornments. 'The explanation of clothes then would tie up with the explanation of body painting, tattooing, tooth-capping and other practices through which man attempts to improve or change his appearance and his presence' (Bate 1952, 101).

During work in the forest, a Koitor's body is exposed to heat from the sun and to the various shades in the forest during periods of rest. The bare body exemplifies a sparse material culture which renders their imagination co-extensive with the universe of the forest. When the Koitors participate in festivals, they dress themselves in colourful clothes. The bare body is an identity in nature; it is the receptor of shades, and of changes in the external environment. The body covered with clothes is an identity in cultures; it distinguishes gender and status.

If the body has to be bent for long periods, the back will be unduly strained. To counteract this, the Koitors adopt the following posture: they stand with feet wide apart and back bent forward at a right angle. As a result, they walk with an absolutely erect posture. The Koitors register the seasons on their bodies. Exposure to heat, cold, and moisture gives the skin its dark colour, its thickness, and its soft texture. During summer, water shortage, heat radiation rising up 14 hands high, and the burning surface of the earth inflict heat boils on the body. The feet get burnt and the soles become thick, coarse, and calloused, and the body becomes lean. The work load is the maximum in the summer. Penda plots need to be cut and prepared for sowing; this work is done while standing. During winter, the Koitors bend the body to harvest the crop. On cold winter nights, the Koitors sleep close to the fire. As a result, the chests of some of the Koitors are burnt black. During monsoons the Koitors protect their growing crop from animals who intrude into the penda, and for this, it is necessary for them to move across the village, from home to field and back again. Continuous exposure to water eats into the skin and causes blisters, especially between the toes. All these inscriptions the seasons leave on the body are a consequence of work in a forest landscape.

This contrast between the bare body and the body covered with clothes draws attention to the complementary relation between the sparseness of material culture in the social environment of the Koitors and the abundance and multiplicity of material life in the forest. The density and richness of forest materials continuously provide for daily and ceremonial needs. The abundance of the forest renders the accumulation of surplus unnecessary for long periods of relative hunger.

The forest landscape circumscribes and inscribes the Koitor's body, the leski circumscribes (*valuhtana*) the *jagabhum*, and the Koitors work in the forest and make it accessible for social use. The term *valuhtana* refers to the areas circumscribed while gathering food, when the crop matures, and while hunting. Further, the body is the geometer, the measure of the forest. Heat in summer is measured by the height of the radiation emanating from the ground, in terms of *khuta* (arm's length); the rising level of water during the monsoon is measured in terms of the height of the body—knee deep, waist deep, etc.; slopes and the size of a penda are measured by the amount of work a person can do within a limited time period in the summer. There is no one standard size of a penda; its size is determined as a ratio of the Koitor's capacity for work. The size and shape of a penda is the outer limit of the extension of the human body in space.

Bhuti is understood by the Koitors as a loss of flesh and blood while working in the forest landscape. When no work is done on the penda on account of either illness or *polowa* (days of no work), the lands are left to rest, and it is possible to observe the beginning of their dissolution, as also the working of a life force which animates the forest and regenerates its multiplicity and abundance. This can be explained by the following example.

While chasing a bear from his penda, Navgu stepped on a one-hand span long bamboo stick as thin and pointed as a grass blade. It pierced his right foot diagonally between the heel and ankle bone, because of which Navgu retired from work to rest. After a few days, his foot swelled up like a balloon. The pain was excruciating. Navgu refused to visit the hospital, saying that he would set it right himself. He called for the leski, who gave him herbs to lessen the pain. He allowed the wound to fill with water and pus until the bamboo piece embedded in the flesh started floating. It took him another two days to prepare himself to bear the extreme pain of pulling out the bamboo piece. On the third day, he slowly pressed the bamboo stick from one side of the swelling, until its tip could be seen at the other end of the swollen foot. On the fifth day, he pulled out the stick with a pair of bamboo tongs and the pus flowed out. Thereafter, he used some herbs to heal the wound. Navgu rested for over a month. During this period, his body lost its strength on account of the pain, and the crop was damaged by the growth of weeds. This was loss of *jiwa* to Navgu. When at rest, the self-activity of nature runs its course in the human body as it does in the penda. While it allows for healing on the one hand, it also results in a loss of work and the consequential loss of crop on the other. This is one way in which the loss of crop is the simultaneous loss of jiwa.

Both the human body and the non-human forest are animated by jiwa, the life force generated by the self-activity of nature. It is symbolically represented by Talurmuttee—mother earth—and refers to the unity of elements in landscape nature necessary for the continuity of life itself. In the words of a Koitor elder:

> Let there be no air, all will die, man, animals, and plants included. Although it is possible to survive for some time without water and food, it is not possible to survive without air. Let there be no rains, there will be no crops and no vegetation in the forest. And we will die of starvation.

It is suggested here that man is as much a part of landscape nature as landscape nature is a part of man. This is reflected in the awareness of the Koitors that the elements constituting jiwa are air, water, fire, and earth. The properties of these elements are observed in everyday life, within the frame of a cultivation cycle.

Air (Vari)

It is said that the presence and absence of *vari* (air) determines the weight of the body. The human body weight is on account of the presence of vari in it. By regulating and controlling vari while breathing, the body weight can be controlled. Death is the passing out of air from the body, or, in the Koitors' words, *vari pestu*. A dead man has maximum weight, since there is no vari in the dead body.

The tiredness of the body or of any of its parts is described as *bojha*, that is, weightiness. It is manifested through irregular breathing and panting. The term used to describe this is *doogana*. In contrast, an active body is light in its movement. It requires maximum vari, and therefore there is fast but regulated breathing.

Further, after death (vari pestu), what is left behind in the body is the 'element' water. The body decays because the water in it is unable to convert itself into vari. This material dissolution of the body is described and explained in terms of the observations of daily life—for example, during the monsoon there is slush, when dry solid mud gets mixed with water, and continuous exposure to water in the monsoons causes the human skin to become soft and start peeling. The effects of the water and the monsoon on material life are used as an analogy to explain death.

Water—Aghe

Following the narrative of Talurmuttee, it is said that the creation of Shringarbhum required the draining out of flood waters. Excessive rainfall leading to floods is therefore a reminder of the possibility of returning to this original state. The quality of flowing water in the rivers is thus associated with preventing disaster and washing away destructive forces. It is often said, 'if there were no rivers and rivulets, all the houses would melt into their constituents, that is, mud and wood, and all crops would be destroyed.' Adequate rainfall cleanses, but it is selective in what it takes. It has the quality of purifying and of cooling—*thandae*. It is believed that diseases adhere to the material objects used by a person. Whenever diseases have to be exorcised from the home or from a village, or when any darm has to be pacified, they are taken to the rivers and immersed. The casting away of these objects into the river drives the disease away. Diseases may also be the result of malevolent darm. In such a case, the members of a household or a village may host a meal in the name of the particular darm, leaving behind the leaf-plates and the leftovers on the river bed. It is believed that the river water carries away all that is destructive and malevolent beyond the bhum. The washing of clothes, bathing, and cleaning are all performed in flowing water.

Flowing water is distinguished from still and stagnant water in waterholes, wells, and hand-pumps. Water from these sources is considered to be of doubtful quality. When flowing water is available, the sources of stationary water are not used—development offices often complain that the wells constructed for the Koitors are not used.

The order of preference and priority accorded to the stationary sources of water is based on how the river water is distributed. If it cannot be established or shown that a well or a hand-pump gets its water supply from the river, then that well or hand-pump will hardly be used. Of the various types of stationary water sources, preference is given to the water in the holes dug in sandy river beds. Flowing water is considered so significant that villages are only set up in a place that is near a river or a small stream.

The properties of flowing water are opposed to those of stagnant water. During the monsoon, on account of the undulating terrain, water collects in varying quantities. It loosens mud and creates *chikla* (slush). Stagnant water absorbs and accumulates dirt, which is regarded as a potential source of illness. Chikla is taken care of by rainfall during monsoons; either the rainwater carries it away or the periodicity of rainfall prevents waterlogging for long periods, and exposure to the sun for a day or two dries up the water, leaving the mud behind.

This manner of thinking about water provides a metaphor for understanding the body in health and in sickness. Sweat is regarded as a variation of flowing water. In a healthy body, it is said that 'there is more vari and little water'. Therefore, it is light. A flabby and soft body is, on the other hand, susceptible to illness; it has more water and less vari, and such a body loses lots of water (sweat) after doing only a little work. It is because of excessive stagnant water that dirt is absorbed. This accounts for the flabbiness of the body and explains its susceptibility to disease and illness.

Therefore, it is argued that it is good to sweat to a point where little water remains in the body. With the flowing away of sweat (or the expulsion of excessive water), diseases are washed away. Susceptibility to disease decreases because there is no water to absorb dirt. Whenever a person feels that he is going to fall ill, he says, 'it is good to go and work in the fields, sweat it out and you will be well'. It is also said, in cases of high temperature, that good work and a stomach full of food are essential to get back to normal.

Seasons are also classified according to the degree of wetness. The most important season is the *peer* (monsoon), of which the *adhe* (summers) and *irangam* (winters) are a function. It is therefore important to study adhe and irangam, the hot and cold months, to know how much water will flow in the rivers during the monsoon. This is an important indicator of the monsoons.

Mud, Soil—*Tori*

Tori (mud) is malleable. With the help of water and air, it can be moulded into any form. It is said that if a wet blob of mud is placed on the palm and squeezed by folding the hand into a fist, mud will emerge from the top, from between the fingers, and from the bottom of the closed fist. These are created by the hand folded into a fist. The closing of the fist, or the closed fist, represents the hands of a worker; for a tool is held in the hand before it can be used.

The common element, jiwa, establishes the bare body as an identity in nature and allows an identification with the forest, and vice versa. For the Koitors, the living forest space itself constitutes a body, internally differentiated into human and non-human nature, both of which animate the forest that emerges as a live, pulsating being, a living space, as it were. The human body is physically marked by forests across seasons, and in turn, it establishes its presence in the forest in penda clearings.

The Forest as Living Space: Self-Activity and the 'Depth' of the Forest

As a living entity, the forest universe unfolds a diversity of lifecycles across seasons, independent of the Koitors' labour. The fading in and fading out of the shades of this universe across seasons, from barrenness in summer to colourful abundance during the monsoon and winter, allows it to be seen as a forest scape. This enables a recognition of the self-regeneration of plural life forms, whereby the forest comes alive for the Koitors. We shall see how, as the forest scape comes alive, it acquires a third dimension, its depth, which allows the forest to be viewed as a living space.

The ground is differentiated into several *jagabhums*. Within a jagabhum, several Talurmuttee are distributed over sub-clans. Each jagabhum is a set of forest clearings—*naga* (for village settlement), penda (for cultivation), and *gera* (a patch of forest). The naga is sub-divided into *para*—neighbourhoods. Each neighbourhood has a gera, sub-divided into areas of bamboo forests, teak forests, grazing land, cultivation plots, etc.

The Koitors recognise the self-activity of the forest from its ability to dissolve the boundaries marked by specialised uses and restore its unity. While the process of self-activity has been seen in relation to the cultivation cycle where the forest regenerates on the penda, we should also consider, as proof of the dissolution, another aspect of the self-activity, viz., the longevity of the materials of the forest that are put together to make a dwelling, which also begins to dissolve when abandoned. Longevity is defined in a comparison between the duration over which the dwelling was used and the duration of time over which it dissolved.

The building of a house in the forest involves the selection of materials (mud, bamboo, and elephant grass) from what is available and a site that will be cleared. Men clear a site and dig out mud to make a mud pit. Women fetch water, which they pour into this pit. Thereafter, the pit becomes a convivial place—anyone from the village or from the neighbourhood (men, women, the elderly, and the young) can walk in and churn the earth till it becomes tight, ready for making the house. Blobs of mud are then carried to an adjacent site to build a hut. The walls are rounded at the edges when the shape is rectangular. Its pyramidal roof, the frame of which is bamboo, is thatched with elephant grass or hay.

If looked after well, the hut lasts one generation. However, when left unattended and neglected, it dissolves into its original elements in two years under the influence of forest regeneration across seasons. The self-activity of nature is intelligible in this contiguity of contraries: the work of man and the work of nature. The longevity of an object, the duration of time over which it dissolves, and the duration of time over which the forest regenerates mark the time-frame of the self-activity of landscape nature. Dissolution frames the duration of the lifecycle of materials of the forest.

This is in contrast to laboratory processes which create chemical compounds in enclosed places insulated from the external life-world. These compounds are qualitatively different from the elements that constitute it. The chemical process of transformation of quantity into quality is irreversible; for, when the chemical compound is left unused, it is waste. However, dissolution with reference to the forest indicates reversibility as an aspect of the self-activity of landscape nature. The hut, when untended, dissolves with the growth of the forest into the elements and materials from which it was made.

Thus, in the Koitors' consciousness the cycle begins with the work of clearing the forest and constructing a hut. It ends with the dissolution of the hut and the regeneration of the forest. This return of forests is simultaneously a return to the point of origin. The meaning that this phenomenon holds for the Koitors is that the self-activity of landscape nature is a principle of unity of the empirical and the ideal aspects of the forest living space.

The depth of this space and the foundational characteristic of this unity of the empirical and the ideal comes to be known during hunting and food-gathering. The forest camouflages the co-presence of other living beings in the animal and the plant kingdoms—birds, insects, plants, and herbs—and the co-presence of human and non-human nature. The possibility of losing one's way in the forest, which is always there during a hunt, for example, underlines the significance of this co-presence.

The contrast between the Koitors and the forest is structured in modes by which, during hunting, the Koitors and the animals recognise each other's presence by sight and sound. It is also known in the continuity of exchange between the work of the Koitors and the work of nature. The camouflage in this context is essentially an ordering or a pattern arrangement comprising both the density of vegetation, its varying shades and colours, and the multiplicity of sounds. The activity of hunting is based on the recognition of this order and pattern, and of spotting animals. This requires a keen sense of sight and sound. The hunter must track and identify animals by their pug marks, by the arrangement of fallen leaves, the grass that hides them, by marks on trees, and the shape vegetation acquires in their resting places when disturbed by their movement. This enables a hunter to sense the lurking presence of an animal, on which the success of hunting depends. In a hunt, the recognition of the crucial movement, one that can lead to success, is the moment when auditory and visual perceptions synchronise.

The forest also camouflages the place of work. The cutting of a forest is original or primordial labour. It exposes the forest clearing to light, introduces discontinuity in the forestscape, and uncovers the self-activity of nature. The forest thus animates the Koitors' social and cultural life. It continually fulfils the demands of everyday life. It is capable of sustaining social life, provided that the critical limits of its self-activity are understood as a frame within which the Koitors work and live. In other words, the forest demands a continuous practice of the skill to recognise an order and pattern of social life that keeps close to the elements of nature.

The Forest as Shared Space

As a child grows under the guidance of elders, s/he is familiarised with forest materials. This takes place around the hut and the penda. However, as an adult worker, a Koitor man and woman must move into the forest for hunting and food-gathering, respectively. These activities are fraught with the possibility at all times of getting lost in the forest, through the forgetting of the path (lesna) that it induces. The ability to make one's way in and out of the forest allows them to know its depth. Ignorance of the order and pattern of the camouflage may result in a loss of life. Koitors tell stories of children and adults who lost their way in the forest and perhaps died or were killed by animals. They also tell stories of elders who, having lost their way, were able to find it.

The central problem with regard to moving in a forest is the loss of a sense of direction on account of a loss of the sense of difference between the forestscapes visible to the eye while moving along any single path in a forward direction, and when returning along the same path. These differences can also be described as a difference of views. To be at home in the forest, it is necessary to differentiate between both the views. In the Koitor mind, the owl is the exemplar in this regard. Like an owl, it is necessary to be able to turn one's vision 180 degrees, to know the difference between forward movement and the movement of return.

The differences in the two views of forestscapes arise from the depth of camouflage and its variety in the universe of the forest. The absence of signs of historical activity and the inability to differentiate one view of the forest from another results in the loss of direction. This is captured in the form of lesna, which means a forgetting resulting in a loss of orientation in time and space. Lesna is contrasted with *marng*, which refers to forgetfulness on account of a lapse in memory.

When faced with loss of orientation, the Koitors observe that normal people behave in two ways. A person runs and, depending upon his good luck, he stumbles upon the right path. The Koitors know of several cases when a *Koska* (outsider) panicked and yet succeeded. But Koitors do not approve of this method. They advise that under these circumstances, during the day, one should stand still and try to locate the position of a human settlement by the position of the sun and the direction of smoke (if any is visible), and at night by the position of the moon and the direction from which the sound of drums and songs sung by *ghotul* boys and girls can be heard. At the same time, they advise that an effort be made to differentiate the camouflage in front. This method, which is not known to, or even knowable by, the Koskas, is described below.

When lost in a forest, Koitors are in a position to confront the forest from within. This is a dramatic confrontation, wherein the process of exploration and discovery of one's bearings in the forest universe rests on a relation and coordination between what one sees and what one hears. In a forest, these visual and auditory perceptions do not synchronise instantly; between auditory and visual observations lies the forest camouflage, which conceals the sources of various kinds of sounds—the movement of animals, the wind, of birds, or of falling leaves—which render the forest alive and animate. Every sound emanating from behind the camouflage signifies a lurking presence. On account of these sounds, the vegetation patterns are transformed into a forest of signs, and the eye distinguishes shades and the ears identify movements of animals, of winds, and so on.

Out of this process emerges an awareness of the forest as a living space in its entirety. At this point in time, the sense of separation between the human body and the forest, or between the human and the non-human body of nature, is obliterated and the Koitor is possessed by the forest, as it were. On account of this movement, fear is generated and with it, the animated non-human nature permeates the body of the Koitor. Fear opens up every pore of the body and informs it of the presence of the forest. In other words, the presence of the forest enters the very being of the Koitors. The Koitor loses her/his presence of mind and hence loses the sense of direction along which s/he is to return. The forest appears to 'dissolve' the Koitor's orientation. It is under these circumstances that the Koitors move to a point of rest in order to differentiate the elements in human and non-human nature. Attention is directed to the sounds of the body to distinguish them from the sounds of the forest. This primary differentiation begins when a correlation is established between what is heard and what is seen. As this correlation dawns from within, the knowledge that makes it possible to find one's way out of the forest becomes accessible. The discovery of the forest when one is lost in it includes the discovery of landscape patterns.

It is important to view the forest as a living space, a whole unified by its material diversity as well as by the life force which animates it. This unity has a mobile form. It is a process which transforms the mere physicality of forest materials—the boundaries that differentiate a forest internally dissolve, as it were, to reveal the seamlessness of the work of nature. In other words, this process of dissolution of the material, tangible aspect of the forest expresses the 'being' of the forest. The forest emerges as a vibrant living space. It can induce forgetting and thereby become accessible to the Koitors from within their selves. This presence of the forest unifies diverse times, as the past, the present, and the future merge in the Koitor's consciousness. The forest becomes an embodiment of an ever present beginning. It partakes of the character of an everlasting timeless entity, producing itself within itself by its self-activity.

Aspects of the Cult of Talurmuttee

The symbol of this unity in Shringarbhum is the abode of mother earth, named as Talurmuttee. Shringarbhum is the very body of Talurmuttee, whose altar is made at the foot of the sal tree. The term 'talurmuttee' literally means *talu*, that is, mother, and *mutte*, or old woman.

When the Koitors are asked, who is Talurmuttee, they pick up some tori (mud, topsoil earth), the empirical referent of Talurmuttee. They say that this is the ground in which the tree is rooted. Tori can be given any number of forms. This, for the Koitors, is exemplified in the diversity of the plants which are a part of the Shringarbhum. The Koitor believes that a tree is the primary manifestation of the self-activity of nature, and thus it forms the site for the altar of Talurmuttee. The differentiation between the various parts of a tree is explained by Koitors through the following example:

> Take mud and mix it with water, or take wet mud (during the monsoon), keep this blob on the palm of the hand, fold the fist tight, then the mud comes out from between the fingers on the side, on top, and at the bottom. The mud in the upper part of a fist signifies the top of the tree; the mud that remains on the palm signifies the trunk, the mud that flows out from between the fingers signifies the leaves and fruits, and the mud that comes out from the bottom signifies the roots. The tight fist signifies the grip of an axe used for cutting a tree.

The camouflage, its density, and variety of life-forms is a symbol of the self-activity of nature. This underlines the economy of nature, which shapes the nature of economy in the forest. For example, it provides for the many needs of the Koitors through the several uses that its materials can be put to. For example, bamboo is used to make homes, fences, bows, arrows, containers, the roof of a hut, and so on.

The work of nature is intelligible in the contrast between types of land: *hema* lands, on which the forest returns when it is left fallow, are opposed to the *pariya* land, on which the forest does not return when it is left fallow. Consequently, the contrast between hema lands and pariya lands distinguishes the work of nature from the work of man. In the former, there is a contiguity, and in the latter, there is a disjunction between fields, fallow land, and forest.

The contiguity between the work of man and the work of nature is at the same time a contiguity between light and shade. For example, as already stated, clearing a patch of forest for cultivation exposes that patch of land to direct sunlight. But the regeneration of forests covers it again with shade. The alternation between light and shade takes place along two axes: (*i*) in their temporal contiguity on a plot; and (*ii*) in their spatial contiguity between a plot and its neighbouring forests. In both cases, the patch of clearing reverts to its forest universe.

The Koitors explain these relations through an analogy with a tree and its relations to its shade (darm), when exposed to light and heat (adhe) from the sun (*pord*). The Koitors use the term darm to describe 'shade', literally as well as metaphorically.

Literally speaking, darm is the dark region on the ground contiguous with an object directly exposed to sunlight. Accordingly, both the tree and the human body have their respective darm. Their difference is intelligible in their relationship to heat and light. The body loses its shadow when it moves away from the sun into the shade of a tree. Here, the human body and the tree are similar in the sense that both have shadows. Their shades, however, signal differences.

This is to say that when exposed to light, the body is in direct relation to adhe (heat) from the sun, which it absorbs. But in the shade of a tree, it is in indirect relation to it, and thus loses heat and cools down. During work, the Koitors describe this contrast as '*adhe verrtu darm dyee*' ('heat has increased, move into the shade'). They stop work on penda plots and move into the shade of a tree to take rest. Here, the porous human body absorbs heat from the sun when at work to clear the forest. The Koitor can see their own shadow on this clearing on the ground, and the shape and size of the clearing itself is a 'shade' on the landscape made by the Koitor's work.

During rest when a Koitor steps into the shade of trees, his body loses its own shadow. There, the body cools down and reinvigorates itself. Heat is contrasted with coolness, as adhe is contrasted with darm; and work is contrasted with rest and play. When the Koitors rest, free from work, they stay in the shade of trees, partaking of the self-activity of nature to invigorate themselves.

So far the physical aspects of shade or darm have been described. The magical and symbolic aspects are highlighted in the work of the leski (a ritual specialist), described in the next section. This aspect is derived from the disjunction of a body from its darm at death. The body is buried and subsequently it dissolves into the earth, but the darm of a person continues to exist in the air. All these darms have a magical effect on the person on whom they fall. This can result in illness and disease, or can enter the body of a leski to possess him and imbue him with special knowledge. The Koitors can use the various names of darms in the practice of *hode*, a black craft, to harm rivals by causing the darm to enter their bodies and make them ill.

In these two different uses—by the leski and the practitioners of hode—the name of a darm has magical qualities, insofar as its utterance is capable of inducing physical changes in the body of the person towards whom the hode is directed. The task of the leski is to identify from these symptoms the particular darm which has been inflicted upon the person's body.

Rest, Work of Nature, and the Leski

In the oral history of the Koitors, the past is framed in dreamtime and is beyond the grasp of everyday life, because the forest merges the past and the present. For instance, when the Kokameta Koitors moved from Jagdalpur to Kokameta via Neygameta, the abandoned settlement returned to its forest universe. While the Koitors from Kokameta can visit relatives in Jagdalpur and Neygameta, they cannot go backwards in this direction to construct a new settlement. It is believed that such a return to the past will result in death.

The Koitors in fact believe that afflictions (*dukhi*) come from the past, camouflaged by the forest. This belief is spatially represented in the practice of *urvna*, an elementary healing practice. The patient sits with his back to the direction of Jagdalpur and his legs stretched flat on the ground. In an attempt to send away the affliction, the leski blows over the patient's body from head to toe, from the back (*poron*) to the front (*irta*).

A different knowledge of the past is accessible to a *pattari*, who sings songs and tells stories and riddles to describe past social lives. He sings for two or more nights during festivals.

The knowledge of a leski and a pattari is not acquired in apprenticeship. It comes to them in dreamtime. This knowledge remains within his *hanal*, the earthen pot of the ancestors. The leski and the pattari differ in the skills they use to illuminate the universe of the past. It is not possible for any non-specialist to know of the path taken in both perspectives, viz., of the forward movement of memory towards the immediate social circumstances, and its movement of return towards the past, that is, of forgetting one's present social being.

The leski uses his skill, lesna, to induce kanjkar, that is, dreamtime, to forget his social being. The pattari sings at night when darkness covers all differences of the social life of daytime, as the Koitors assemble in a shared place. The specialised lineages of leski and pattari relate to dreamtime in a complementary way, to cover the universe framed by it: the leski by 'inducing forgetting', and the pattari, by remembering. The knowledge of the past is differentiated socially between the Koitors (the non-specialists), the pattari, and the leski (the specialist).

Forgetting is a form of dissolution and is distinct from forgetfulness caused by a lapse of memory. The latter introduces discontinuities in social life, expressed as a misunderstanding, or indiscretion on account of either failure of communication or excess of communication; a lapse of memory is an attribute of a historical psyche (Levi-Strauss

1985, 413). In contrast, a leski exercises his discretion to induce forgetting, and a pattari does not forget what he learns in kanjkar. In the former, forgetting and remembering are complementary; in the latter, forgetfulness and memory are the antithesis of each other.

A leski prevents the dissolution of work on the fields by the self-activity of the forest, because by curing illness, he enables the Koitor to return to work. He mediates between work and rest.

A leski is skilled in inducing a forgetting of his social being, and stepping into a kanjkar or dreamtime analogous to the self-activity of the forest. The emphasis is on sleep time, when dreams fade in and fade out of their own accord. The literal meaning of the term lesna, his skill, is to forget, in the sense, lose track of. By the practice of his skills, he dissolves the awareness of his self as a member of a household, clan, lineage, or a village in order to enter Shringarbhum, or allow it to enter him. The skill comes to him by reason of his membership of a particular hanal. It cannot be learnt in apprenticeship, or as a part of the general process of socialisation. Consequently, the skill disappears after death, only to reappear in sleep or dreamtime to any one of his deserving descendants. When and to whom it returns cannot be known. The Koitors point out that this may take two to three generations. Since this skill disappears with death and reappears on its own accord, it is a sensible form of the self-activity of nature.

This is best demonstrated at the time of *penu-kaksar*. These are clan festivals, when the relationship between the social being of the Koitors and the specialised skill of a leski is discernible as play. On this occasion, a leski gets possessed of his own accord. In the course of conversation, his body begins to tremble from foot to head. This magnifies into larger movements and loud sounds. The leski's voice changes, his eyes are half-closed, and the language he speaks changes; although he speaks in the local dialect, its phonetic flow is altered by rapid speech. This is described as *kaksar* or play.

As a part of this play, a leski uses whips tipped with sharp rusted iron nails to beat his own body; he sits on a seat made of iron nails; he pierces his cheeks with iron rods. Although his skin peels off and bleeds, the wounds do not get infected. This severance of the leski self from his body lies at the root of kanjkar. The Koitors consider this a proof of his powers and of truth, the *sat* of kanjkar.

A new leski presents himself for recognition on the day of kanjkar. The Koitors know that several individuals pretend to be possessed, imitating the body of a leski. To distinguish a true leski from frauds, other leski present on the occasion are consulted. They ask several questions to find out if any one of his ancestors had been a leski, failing which other tests are resorted to. The surest of them all is to ask the leski to beat himself, or hold a burning piece of wood, or to prove his powers by curing an illness.

As a part of the lore on leski, the elders in Kokameta describe some tests performed in the past. On one occasion, all the leskis of the region were assembled. A pile of dry chillies was burnt and they were asked to inhale the smoke. Only one could; the others gave up. Accordingly, a gradation was set up to differentiate between the more powerful and less powerful leskis. To determine this gradation, the elders in Kokameta describe similar tests performed in the past.

With his knowledge and skill, a leski manipulates materials like water, *agarbatti* (incense sticks), incense, rice, and turmeric, and uses an incantation to induce the forgetting of his social being by entering kanjkar. When he emerges from kanjkar, he is unable to recollect what he had said while he was in it. In relation to the phenomenon of fading out of his social being and the fading in of kanjkar, lesna is translated as 'forgetting'.

When in kanjkar, what a leski sees or views or knows is recognised from the names he calls. These, the Koitors point out, refer to the shades (darm) and shapes of the past, camouflaged by the self-activity of the forests and identified by the mind when it becomes self-active in kanjkar. The differences between leski are manifest from the differences in their gait and their respective *parde*, that is, the tunes and drum beats played by the *mohiria* and the *nagrche* (musicians who belong the Panka clan), respectively.

The leski uses special terms to call darms onto himself to cure dukhi. These terms therefore offer descriptions of the internality of objects or of their life-force. The Koitors explain this internality by an analogy: just as wood burns because there is fire in it and floats because it is in its nature to do so, in a similar way the quality internal to objects is known to all from their use in social life. Although the names of dukhi are public knowledge, other names of gods and goddesses, of medicinal plants and roots, and their use is secret knowledge.

The Merging of Past, Present, and Future

The birth of a child is marked by a period of isolation for the mother, the father, and the newborn. This period is considered liminal and inauspicious because the child may or may not survive. It is kept out of sight to prevent an evil eye from being cast on it. If the child survives, s/he is ceremonially given social membership first, as an ancestor. Women from the immediate households of both parents gather to discover which ancestor has been born in the person of the child. They place in the hands of the child a few grains of rice. It is then addressed by kin terms—*tado*, *bapi*, *ako*, *kako*, which refers to father's father, father's mother, mother's father, and mother's mother, respectively. The term for which the child closes its fist is the category of the ancestor reborn. The child represents a continuity of the dead with the living, and of the past with the present.

The Koitor's understanding of temporality unfolds the origins of Shringarbhum. This, according to the epic of Talurmuttee, is when the water that submerged Shringarbhum was distributed into waterways and water bodies, disclosing the universe of the forest as a living space. Accordingly, the age of a hanal is directly determined by the number of generations that have passed. Those born first are younger because they are closer to the point of origin, and those born later are elders because they are farther from the point of origin. Time is understood from the points of the beginning of Shringarbhum. This underlines the birth of a child as a mythic and extraordinary event. The reckoning of time takes into account the origin of Shringarbhum for purposes of placing each generation within the frame of the long duration. In this mode of reckoning time, Koitors are able to constantly remind themselves of this mythic and extraordinary event. In this mode, the actual time that has passed between the origin of Shringarbhum and the present is also dissolved. Like the self-activity of the forests and the induced forgetting of a leski, the set of four terms offered to a child to begin its social membership constitutes the mnemonics of 'induced forgetting'. On the one hand, it reduces the population of the living and the dead to four categories, and on the other, it opens and closes a unit of three generations within which all differentiations take place.

A Thought for Reflection

The differentiation and togetherness of humans and non-human nature in the universe of the forest underlines the significance of what is worthy of forgetting and what is worthy of remembering, not only for Koitor social life but also for social life as such.

Endnote

1. This chapter is from my doctoral thesis, 'A Study in the Sociology of Agriculture', submitted to the Department of Sociology, Delhi University, January 1991.

three

Instrumental Labour Teleology

PESA 1996 and FRA 2006*

Today, in 2023, the urgency to safeguard the health of planet Earth and our sanity as its inhabitants requires measures to reorient economic development to, *first*, not damage whatever remains of natural landscapes, and *second*, to enrich the economy with livelihoods that do not undermine the processes rejuvenating landscape diversity. The legitimacy for this reorientation is provided by a new normative of justice: what is unjust for human beings cannot be just for the 'being of natural landscapes'. For instance, the injustice from violence between human beings cannot be just for 'the being of natural landscapes' because these are also its victims. Similarly, what is not just for the 'being of landscapes' cannot be just for human beings. For instance, the injustice of fencing seamless natural landscapes or reckless deforestation cannot be just for human beings who are displaced by it.

This reorientation will require labour teleology to be aligned to 'natural landscapes'. The labour teleology of the contemporary modern political economy is aligned to abstract nature, and is destructive of the

*An earlier version of this chapter was published as 'PESA 1996: De-centering the Political Economy', in Samuel Berthet and Girish Kumar (eds), *New States for a New India: Federalism and Decentralization in the States of Jharkhand and Chhattisgarh*. New Delhi: Manohar, 2011.

Parts of this chapter have also been published earlier as 'Forest Rights Act 2006: Undermining the Foundational Value of the forest', in *The Economic and Political Weekly* XLVI (15), 9 April 2011.

being of natural landscapes. Regimes of production and reproduction cut large forest areas in the name of economic development and evict communities dwelling in forests. After decades of environmental activism and public education, regimes have been invented to compensate for the destruction of forests for economic development by planting trees elsewhere and by efforts to rehabilitate to evicted communities. Over time, these compensation regimes have become perverse incentives for deforestation, undermining the integrity of the being of natural landscapes and of human beings, rendering the conflicts between human beings and landscapes intractable.

This chapter argues that PESA (Panchayats Extension to Scheduled Areas Act), 1996 and FRA (Forest Rights Act), 2006 are instances of such perverse political economy. These have marginalised reflexive labor. Both these Acts are designed to provide compensation to tribal forest dwellers. PESA has no provision for rights over land or livelihood; it has provisions for rehabilitation against land acquisition for non-forest activity (economic development). FRA seeks to correct this with provisions for forest rights (individual and community).

The first part of this chapter discusses labour teleology aligned with abstract nature. The second and third parts discuss PESA 1996 and FRA 2006 as expressions of this labour teleology.

Labour Teleology Aligned to Abstract Nature

Labour teleology, as discussed by Lukacs (1980 [1978]) in his work, 'On Labour and the Ontology of Social Being', has three aspects: *first*, it changes the form of natural materials and introduces a break in the contiguity of the work of nature and the work of human beings. This pulls the social being from mere nature-boundedness.

> .... what distinguishes the worst architect from the best of bees is that the architect builds the cells in his mind before he constructs it in wax. At the end of every labour process, a result emerges which had been conceived by the worker at the beginning, hence already existed ideally. Man not only effects a change of form in the materials of nature; he also realises his own purpose in those materials. (ibid., 3)

Second, it tries to secularise the world by creating a dichotomy between the ideal and the real.

> Every teleological process involves the positing of a goal, and therefore a goal positing consciousness .... with this act of positing, consciousness initiates a real process, precisely a teleological one.... The teleological conception of nature and history .... implies that this existence and movement must have a conscious creator both in overall process and in its details.... The need that gives rise to conceptions of the world .... to make sense of existence, from the course of the world, down to the experiences of individual life.... Even after the development of the sciences demolished that religious ontology .... this primitive and elementary need survived.... (Lukacs (1980 [1978], 5)

Third, the teleology determines labour as subject and nature as object.

> ... we seek to find meaning and justification. As if things were so ordained that everything that happens must have a meaning. (ibid., 6)
>
> ... Through labour, a teleological positing is realised within the material being, as the rise of a new objectivity.... labour becomes the model for any social practice, for in such social practice .... teleological positings are always realised ... materially. (ibid., 3)
>
> ... for Marx labour is not one of the many phenomenological forms of teleology in general, but rather the only point at which a teleological positing can be ontologically established as a real moment of material actuality ... that all labour would be impossible if it were not preceded by a positing of this kind, one that determined its process at every step.... (ibid., 8–9)
>
> The positing of the goal arises from a human social need; yet in order to be a genuine positing of a goal, investigation of the means, i.e., knowledge of nature, must have reached a certain appropriate level; if it has not, then the positing of this goal remains merely a utopian project, a kind of dream.... Thus the point at which labour connects with the rise of scientific thought and its development from the standpoint of ontology of being is precisely the region described as the investigation of the means.... (ibid., 15)

At the turn of the twenty-first century, labour teleology positioned genocide, ecocide in contiguity with economic development across the world (Padel and Das 2006). The forest has been removed from its foundational position in the order of things in the world, with far-reaching consequences.

The deforested being of all things living in this world is left unsheltered, displaced, dislocated, and vulnerable. There is unprecedented loss of resilience, colossal irreversible damage to forest materials, destruction of peoples' livelihoods, liquidation of their sense of belonging, obliteration of identity, and impairment of forest-based ecosystems across the world.

There is a finality that is built into labour teleology. The value created by labour time cannot provide a forest canopy for the 'unsheltered being', and there is no way in which the value created in the market can determine the depth and scale of the colossal loss. What does the vulnerability of a deforested being suggest about value? What holds up the being of living things in the face of the possibility of an absolute collapse of being itself? Some examples can help us to ponder upon these questions.

What is the value of the position of pillar(s) that keep a building from falling; the position of the backbone that holds up the human skeleton? Shifting the pillar or the backbone from their respective positions in the structure and/or the use of inappropriate materials to make them will result in the crumbling of the structure. The position of the pillar in relation to the position of other parts of a building and of the backbone in relation to other parts of the skeleton is a 'foundational structural position'. This position has foundational value. It determines what material is appropriate and how much of it is adequate to make the pillar and the backbone. Together, the position and the material keep the structure firmly grounded, give it strength, build its resilience, make it resistant to external pressure, and through all this, bring to its being-in-the-world a 'presence'.

Thus the 'value of the foundational position' derives from the mode of being in the world and also belongs to it.

Deforestation undermines the value of this position; the significance of the forest puts it in this position. When the forest is in its foundational position, it brings animals, plants, and human beings together to frame the objective conditions for the being of things living in the world. All living beings, irrespective of their physical distance from the forest, belong to it. The forest thus has a significant 'presence' in the order of things in this worldview. To be at home inside, and to not be alienated when outside, the forest, it is necessary to belong to the 'presence of the forest'. In the absence of such belonging, being inside the forest is as good as being outside it.

Those who live in the forest and others outside it—either in its immediate neighbourhoods or far away in the rural areas and cities—could belong to this presence on the condition that the co-presence of human and non-human nature, which resides in both human and non-human living beings, is acknowledged and accepted as an indispensable condition for being in the world. This worldview is then based on the principle of coexistence of all living and non-living beings.

Marx's labour theory of value can help us understand this worldview. In principle, there is contiguity between the work of nature and the work of human beings. The former cannot be exchanged and this is a basic condition, for this labour gives it its foundational position. It is neither subject nor object. The latter can be exchanged. Thus, the work of nature is positioned as the foundation for the work of human beings. The relation of contiguity determined that the value created from the investment of labour time is different from, but contiguous with, the value of all natural materials which have not been created by the investment of human labour

This contiguity is the basis for coexistence. Labour teleology in fact breaks this contiguity by shifting the presence of the forest from its foundational position.

PESA 1996

This section discusses PESA 1996 (for details, see Appendix 1) in the Fifth Schedule Areas: Andhra Pradesh, Bihar, Gujarat, Himachal Pradesh, Maharashtra, Madhya Pradesh, Odisha, and Rajasthan, Chhattisgarh, and Jharkhand.

PESA 1996 has four sections, with a total of twenty-four provisions. Of these, there are fifteen main provisions (arranged alphabetically from 'a' to 'o') and nine sub-provisions. Section 4 empowers tribal people with decision-making powers. One set of four provisions comprises two sections, (a) and (b), which are concerned with traditions and customs, and sections (c) and (d), which define the Gram Sabha as a body of persons included in the electoral rolls for the Panchayat, and detail its powers to safeguard these traditions and customs.

The second set of twenty sections positions the Gram Sabha in the modern political and economic system. Section 4(e) has two sub-provisions (i–ii), which bring the Gram Sabha concerned with economic development. Section 4(g) is concerned with the reservation of seats; Section 4(i) discusses the need to consult the people before land acquisition and before resettlement or rehabilitation. Section 4(k) states that mining will be carried out with the recommendation of the Gram Sabha. Section 4(m) has seven sub-provisions (i–vii): here, the Gram Sabha is given powers to own minor forest produce, prevent land alienation, manage village markets, control moneylending, institutions, functionaries, local plans, etc. (see Appendix 1, for PESA).

However, the historical background of these two sets of provisions is different. The first set is concerned with the traditions and customary practices of people, and needs to be viewed in the backdrop of the recorded long history of tribal movements. To begin with, the 110 known instances of assertion over a period of 117 years, from 1783 to 1900 (Guha 1983, 13) were muted when the British classified them as insurgents and segregated them from the rest of India into excluded and partially excluded areas.

Alongside, there emerged a political vanguard who took it upon themselves to articulate, on behalf of the people, their problems and woes. From the early 1940s to the 1950s–1960s, the Communist vanguard mobilised peasants and tribals around land alienation. Some of these issues related to zamindari abolition, land reform and land redistribution, and the chronic food crisis. In the decade of the late 1960s and mid-1970s, that is, between the rise of the Naxalbari uprising in Bengal and the national Emergency, there was an unprecedented shift in the contours of the land question. The government undertook land acquisition for mining, mega-hydroelectric dams, nuclear plants, missile launching stations, nature reserves, etc., displacing large populations of tribal people in the process, with no prospects for rehabilitation. We know that statistically, the tribes are the largest population group to have been displaced in the post-independence history of India.

The demand for redistribution was rendered meaningless. Land was no longer just a means of production, it was now a site for forest and river biodiversity as well as a landscape for tribal modes of living in a world where human and non-human beings live side by side.

On the one hand, there was disillusionment with the political economy of development and on the other, with the decline of institutional politics. The led to a change in vanguard, and four distinct political processes became noticeable. All of them moved away from and critiqued the elite version of history and society. *First* came the vanguard of the militant political left, which emerged with the Naxalbari uprisings and grew steadily aggressive, over time spreading to make up what is now known as the Red Corridor. They moved into the forest, mobilised the tribals to take up arms, and ensured a total closure of any development programmes. Other than their violent confrontations with police and the army, there is little information in the public domain on how they treated the tribal people. They are of the view that the culture of tribal people did not possess any transformative potential. *Second*, there emerged a vanguard of university intellectuals, inspired by Ranajit Guha from Cambridge University.

> … An assortment of marginalised academics—graduate students yet to complete their dissertation, two or three very young scholars only recently admitted to the teaching profession, and an older man stuck at its lowest rung apparently for good—had the advantage of owing no loyalty to any department, faculty, school or party. With no curriculum, no dogma, no official line to guide, no professor, no prophet, or politburo to watch its every step…. (Chatterjee 2013 [2010], 323–324)

These were 'urban intellectuals who had an intense attraction for the rural' (ibid., 13).

Ranajit Guha argued that tribals are not a pre-political people, nor are they revolutionaries in the manner conceptualised by European Marxist thinkers such Antonio Gramsci, amongst others. His understanding resonates with the understanding of the left militants of the Red Corridor, namely that people's cultural language and idioms lack transformative potential. He did not critique the praxis of left militancy. His understanding of praxis drew on the work of semiotics and Marxist writings to illuminate the consciousness of a 'mass of the labouring population and the intermediary strata in towns and country—that is, the people' (Chatterjee 2013 [2010], 323). This 'text view' perhaps needs to be supplemented and complemented with a field view, to provide a holistic understanding.

Third, there emerged approximately 20,000–30,000 groups (Seth 2014, 105) that constituted non-political party micro-movements existing on the periphery of electoral systems. These became politically visible, differentiating themselves firmly from welfare and philanthropic non-political NGOs, as well as from political parties and several mass-based movements of protest (for a detailed discussion, see Seth 2014). The lineage of these groups has been traced to Gandhian, socialist, communist, and social reform movements.

The *fourth* strand emerged with Adivasi community assertions, which demonstrated transformative possibilities. This proved the subaltern vanguard wrong (who believed, as mentioned earlier, that cultural idioms were devoid of any transformative potential) and enriched the non-party political process by collaborating with non-Adivasi people on the one hand while keeping a distance from the militant left on the other. Briefly, community assertions have been able to successfully stop the construction of dams on the Koel and Karo rivers in Jharkhand and bauxite mining in the Nyamgiri hills of Odisha. In both instances, they have refused to align with the Maoists.

Of these four, the efforts of non-party mobilisations led to the inclusion of the first set of provisions (referred to above) in the PESA.

> The Bharat Jan Andolan (BJA), an organization formed by B.D. Sharma on 2 November 1991, tirelessly worked for the cause of a separate panchayat extension law for the SAs. It played a central role in the formation of National Front for Adivasi Self-rule (NFASR)

> in 1994, constituted by many grassroots tribal organizations. Due to continuous pressures from the BJA and other local tribal organizations, the GoI formed a committee in June 1994 to consider the different aspects for a law to extend the Panchayati Raj to the SAs. Headed by Dilip Singh Bhuria, with the BJA leader B.D. Sharma as one of its members, the committee submitted its report in January 1995. Many states, however, were conducting elections in SAs on the basis of their respective Panchayati Raj Acts. The BJA and other organizations challenged it in the court and after the submission of Bhuria Committee Report, the Hyderabad High Court postponed the panchayat elections in the SAs of Andhra Pradesh. The Patna High Court too accepted that such a routine extension would violate the Constitution and underlined that the Parliament would need to enact a special law for the SAs.... The NFASR intensified its movement for the enactment of a separate law for the extension of Panchayati Raj in the SAs.... Ultimately, due to immense pressure of people's movement, the PESA was passed by the Parliament on 24 December 1996, ... based on the recommendations of the Bhuria Committee. (https://www.mha.gov.in/sites/default/files/PESAAct1996_0.pdf, 7–8)

The second set of provisions in the PESA synchronised with changes in the global context. India was of critical importance in the objective conditions created by the World Trade Organization (WTO) neo-liberalisation of economies across the world. The crisis in the world economy in the latter half of the twentieth century—the 1970s and 1980s—on account of an alarming depletion of the natural resource base, amongst other things, led to a paradigmatic transformation of production lines. National boundaries were opened up to aid the speedy movement of factors of production. Faster technologies were introduced. Transnational commodity chains started to govern the international market and determine the relations of production. In this context, a new GATT (General Agreement on Tariffs and Trade) arrangement at the Uruguay Round of GATT negotiations took place in 1986.

Statecraft in India gradually began to function in accordance with these developments by creating commensurate legal regimes. In 1986, India opposed the setting up of these new GATT arrangements

(Devdutt 2002, 74–75). However, in 1989, the Government of India had to agree to these new arrangements, which were to include agriculture and intellectual property rights, amongst other things (ibid.). That same year, with the smashing of the Berlin Wall, the war between the economies of the free market and State-planned communist economies turned in favour of the former. This sped up the Uruguay round[1] of talks, which then moved on to the formation of the WTO in 1995.

Simultaneously in India, in 1986 the L. M. Singhvi Committee submitted its report recommending constitutional status for panchayats. In 1988, the Parliament Consultative Committee appointed a sub-committee under the chairmanship of P. K. Thungon to consider a constitutional amendment. On 15 May 1989, the Constitution (64th Amendment) Bill was introduced in Parliament.[2] Although the Constitution Bill won a two-thirds majority in the Lok Sabha, it failed in the Rajya Sabha. In 1991, the Indian government formulated its New Economic Policy and the Congress Party government introduced the 73rd (Panchayats) and 74th (Municipalities) Constitutional Amendment Bills, which were passed in both chambers in December 1992 as the 73rd and 74th Amendment Acts, respectively, and came into force in 1993. In 1995, four years after the New Economic Policy, India became the founder-member of the WTO.

Amongst other things, these changes launched the Indian economy on the path of neo-liberalisation (Nayar 1998). PESA was enacted in 1996 (within the frame of the 73rd Amendment) only a year after India became the founding member of WTO. Seen in this perspective, PESA is an instrument of the neoliberal economy that was then beginning to take shape. It opened the way for neoliberal capital to reach the tribal villages. In the discussion that follows, the significance of these two aspects of PESA will be examined in relation to the State and in relation to the four political processes discussed above.

With regard to the neoiberal political economy, it was stipulated that if the Fifth Schedule states had not adopted PESA as required by law within one year, it would become automatically applicable. The State needs to make appropriate amendments in their laws/Acts which impinge on the specific provisions contained in the Central Act, namely (*i*) Land Acquisition Act; (*ii*) Excise Act; (*iii*) State Irrigation Act; (*iv*) Minor Forest Produce Act; (*v*) Mines and Minerals Act; (*vi*)

TABLE 3.1. NOTIFIED FIFTH SCHEDULE AREAS

States	PESA District (both partly and fully covered)	PESA District (fully covered)	PESA District (partly covered)
Andhra Pradesh	5	0	5
Madhya Pradesh	20	5	15
Chhattisgarh	19	13	6
Maharashtra	12	0	12
Gujarat	11	4	7
Odisha	13	6	7
Himachal Pradesh	3	2	1
Rajasthan	5	2	3
Jharkhand	16	13	3
Telangana	4	0	4

Source: MOPR, Government of India (accessed 20 October 2017).

Land Revenue Cod/Act; (*vii*) SC/ST Land Alienation Act; (*viii*) Money Lenders Act; and (*ix*) Regulated Market Act (see Table 3.1).

In all nine states, the demographic structure is not in favour of the tribal population (see Table 3.4). What will the dynamics be? Which sections of non-tribals will offer support? And who will stand to benefit?

Reports from different parts of India provide a glimpse of the dynamics. Rajasthan amended its state laws only in 1999. As Ginny Shrivastava, coordinating director, Aastha Sansthan, a not-for-profit organisation assisting tribals in Rajasthan since 1986, says:

> The way the state government has formulated the provisions, it does not translate into the tribal villagers getting their rights; the rights over minor forest produce (MFP) for instance. Though the tribals are supposed to own MFP, they are sometimes forbidden from collecting it and the rights are auctioned off to others. (Ghosh 2007)

S. Upadhyay (2004) 'delves in some detail into the manner in which the States' have subverted the mandate of the Central Legislation (PESA) by carefully using the wordings in law to make

Table 3.2. Comparison of State-wise Percentage of Scheduled Tribes, Census 2001–Census 2011

State/UT Code	India/States/ Union Territory	Percentage of Scheduled Tribes, 2001			Percentage of Scheduled Tribes, 2011		
		Total	Rural	Urban	Total	Rural	Urban
	India	8.2	10.4	2.4	8.6	11.3	2.8
2	Himachal Pradesh	4	4.3	1.3	5.7	6.1	2.6
8	Rajasthan	12.6	15.5	2.9	13.5	16.9	3.2
10	Bihar	0.9	1	0.5	1.3	1.4	0.6
20	Jharkhand	26.3	31	9.8	26.2	31.4	9.8
21	Odisha	22.1	24.6	8.1	22.8	25.7	8.5
22	Chhattisgarh	31.8	37.6	8.4	30.6	36.9	10
23	Madhya Pradesh	20.3	25.8	4.9	21.1	27.2	5.2
24	Gujarat	14.8	21.6	3.2	14.8	23.1	3.5
28	Andhra Pradesh	6.6	8.4	1.8	7	9.3	2.4

Source: Government of India 2013, 126.

the implementation vague and ineffective, especially in the context of 'community resources' in Scheduled Areas.

> The control over prospecting of minor minerals, planning and management of water bodies, control and management of minor forest produce, prevention of alienation of land are all subject to rules in force or as may be prescribed by the State. The fact that the enabling rules are not in place even more than eight years after the adoption of the central law on PESA suggests reluctance by the State Governments to operationalise the mandate of PESA.
>
> There are four points that need particular emphasis here. First there are critical omissions of the fundamental principles of Adivasi livelihoods, without which the spirit of PESA can never be realized. Secondly, the state legislations, perhaps by design, has taken away powers from the traditional Adivasi Gram Sabha which is a collective of all village people. The empowerment of Adivasi gram sabhas is most important for making local self-governance a reality, especially in relation to managing common pool resources. Thirdly, even where it affirmed some provisions of the law in principle, their applicability was made subject to framing of rules/orders or 'as may be prescribed.' As stated earlier, such enabling rules are not yet in place in most cases. Finally, few rules and prescriptions began to surface primarily through revocable official circulars but have been totally inoperative because of the ambiguity and lack of clarity of these provisions. Thus, a promising radical law has been reduced largely to a paper law.

In 2006, a sub-committee set up by the Planning Commission stated that in Raigarha, the grey areas are:

> Denial of gram sabha resolutions; Land acquisition without appropriate consultation with gram sabha; tribal land alienation; acquisition and/or encroachment on common property resources i.e. land, forest and water bodies; violations of human rights; lack of knowledge about PESA at village and administrative level; significant numbers of pending cases in lower courts and at administrative level; lack of transparency on land acquisition/purchasing; Lack of rehabilitation of project affected population; no compensation for landless. (Planning Commission 2006, 138)

These grey areas have not been created by bad governance and cannot be resolved by good governance, which is understood as the proper implementation of the laws. In fact, these grey areas are non-compliances, which can be taken to the court by the Gram Sabha. In the legislation, no clause deters or penalises non-compliance.

Upadhyay rightly argues that the terms 'consultation' and 'as may be prescribed' make PESA an instrument of State regulation. He argues that these terms go against the spirit of PESA. He suggests that we think about why 'consultation' is preferred over 'consensus': 'The use of the word "consultation" under PESA instead of "consent" significantly waters down the power vested with the Panchayat.' In a consultation in the context of PESA, ideas, opinions, views, questions, and stands exchanged are not binding; this refers to a body of knowledge and information which may or may not be applied, used, or brought before any competent authority.

For instance, Upadhayay (2004) points out,

> In Maharashtra the power to consult before land acquisition has been granted to every Panchayat i.e. at Gram Panchayat, Panchayat Samiti and Zila Parishad level (all tiers of local self-government)—provided that, every Panchayat shall consult the Gram Sabha before conveying its views to the Land Acquisition Authority concerned. Note here that there is a provision of 'conveying views' and without any clarity on what happens if such conveyed views are not taken into account.

It can be argued that the absence of any provision for 'conveying views' is part of the definition of consultation. But with the inclusion of such a provision, would consultation not then be a step towards consensus? The phrase 'as may be prescribed' also demonstrates the prerogative of all nine Fifth Schedule states to determine the tone and tenor of the definitions and procedures to be adopted on all subjects listed in PESA (minor forest produce, alienation of land, management of minor water bodies, and control over local plans and their resources) listed in PESA section 4(m). That is to say, the Gram Sabha or the Panchayats at the appropriate level has the power to take decisions, but not to provide appropriate definitions.

In this regard, Upadhyay (2004) points out,

> As per the Central PESA the power to plan and manage 'minor water bodies' exclusively vested with the Panchayat at Appropriate Level (PAL) which in other words means that the Central law gives a discretion to the states to assign to any tier of the local self-government such power in the best interest of the community. However, the first obstacle is on the definition itself. No legal definition of minor water bodies exists in the statute books. The states too have ignored it, whether by design or default is unclear. The Gujarat State in the Western India has given such power to the Gram Panchayat (Village Council). The State of Himachal Pradesh in the north has assigned it to Village Council (Gram Panchayat) OR at Block Committee Level i.e. Panchayat Samiti OR District Council (Zila Parishad) level 'as may be specified'. The State of Rajasthan in the North West too uses the word 'as may be prescribed' by the State.

In 2016, a study undertaken by the Centre for Equity Studies reported that PESA works only in Andhra Pradesh (see Table 3.3).

Nearly twenty-nine years have elapsed, but the task of bringing PESA and the state laws in consonance with each other is still incomplete.

It is clear that in several states, the governments are reluctant to operationalise the PESA mandate.

These glimpses merely show the tip of the iceberg and prove that the deep structures of PESA do not safeguard the cultural traditions associated with tribal modes of livelihood. To the contrary, it opens up the land and forest for non-tribal stakeholders by marginalisng tribal traditions of consensual local self-governance. The people can protect and/or defend whatever land they have acquired by means of 'procedures of consensual local self-governance' by making use of the decision-making powers given to them through the electoral process.

PESA and the Four Political Mobilisations

Nandini Sundar (2005) provided a glimpse of the significance of PESA in relation to the four political mobilisations (discussed above):

Table 3.3. Working of Relevant Laws in Indian States (Impressions from research sites)

State	Main Protective Law (and its working)	Main Restorative Law (and its working)	PESA 1996 (its working)	FRA 2005 (its working)
Andhra Pradesh	AP Scheduled Areas Land Transfer Regulation, 1959	AP Assigned Lands (Prohibition of Transfers) Act, 1977	Yes	Yes
Chhattisgarh	Chhattisgarh Land Revenue Code, 1959	Section 170(B) of Chhattisgarh Land Revenue Code, 1959	No	No
Gujarat	Gujarat Land Revenue Rules, 1972, Sections 73AA, 73AB, 79, its frequently not working, collector openly gives permission for land sale and transfer, even for government land	Very few cases have successful chances of restoring rights to land, and high-profile cases that the tribals oppose have no chance of succeeding.	No	No
Jharkhand	Chota Nagpur Tenancy (CNT) Act, 1908. Santhal Parganas Tenancy Act, 1949, applied to some districts	CNT 1908, Scheduled Areas Regulation, 1969	No	Yes
Madhya Pradesh	Madhya Pradesh Land Revenue Code, 1959	Section 170(B)	No	No
Maharashtra	Maharashtra Land Revenue Code, 1966, Section 36, all the laws are on feet [*sic*] on brokers, corporates,	Maharashtra Restoration of Lands to Scheduled Tribes Act, 1974, is working, but the rate of decline	PESA does not work as a law; from	No

(contd...)

(Table 3.3 contd...)

State	Main Protective Law (and its working)	Main Restorative Law (and its working)	PESA 1996 (its working)	FRA 2005 (its working)
	politicians and government officials	of cases by court and government officials is high	Gram Sabha to government officials, all broke the PESA law	
Odisha	Section 22 of Orissa Land Reforms Act, 1960	Section 23, 23(A), Orissa Land Reforms Act, 1960	No	NA
Rajasthan	Rajasthan Tenancy Act, 1955, Sections 43, 42, 46	Section 183(B), Rajasthan Tenancy Act	No	No
Tripura	Tripura Tribal Areas Autonomous District Council Bill (TTAADC), 1979	Section 187 of Tripura Land Revenue and Land Reforms Act, 1960	No	No

Note: Nearly twenty-nine years have elapsed, but the task of bringing PESA and the state laws in consonance with each other is still incomplete.

Source: Adapted from Mohd., et al. 2016, Annex 4, 273–274, and corrected.

TABLE 3.4. STATE GOVERNMENT LAWS IN COMPLIANCE WITH PESA

States	Land Acquisition	Excise	Forest Produce	Mines and Minerals	Agri-produce Market	Money-lending
Andhra Pradesh	N	N	N	N	N	N
Madhya Pradesh	Y	Y	N	Y	Y	N
Chhattisgarh	Y	Y	N	Y	Y	Y
Maharashtra	N	N	Y	N	N	N
Gujarat	N	Y	N	Y	Y	Y
Odisha	N	Y	Y	Y	N	Y
Himachal Pradesh	Y	Y	Y	Y	N	N
Rajasthan	N	N	N	Y	N	Y
Jharkhand	N	N	Y	N	N	N
Telangana	N	N	N	N	N	N

Note: 'Y' denotes the provision is PESA-compliant; 'N' denotes the provision is not yet PESA-compliant.
Source: Madhu 2017, 88; MOPR, Government of India (accessed 20 October 2017.

On the one side are adivasi groups, like the Jharkhand Pradesh Parha Raja, Manjhi Parganait Manki Munda, Doklo Sohor Maha Samiti, who oppose having elections in scheduled areas. They argue that they are better off with their own customary headmen … than with a three-tier elected system…. They also point to the fact that these customary structures have been recognised in the Chhotanagpur Tenancy Act 1908 (CNTA) and the Santhal Parganas Tenancy Act 1949 (SPTA), and that the Jharkhand Panchayati Raj Act 2001 (PRA) fails to deal with the overlap or contradictions with these laws that might emerge.

On the other side are OBC (mainly Kurmi Mahato) and non-tribal groups like Chatra Yuva Sangharsh Samiti and the Jharkhand Pradesh Panchayatiraj Adhikar Manch (JPPAM), who see no special future for adivasis in Jharkhand. They argue that reserving the chair's seat for adivasis in scheduled areas violates their own citizenship rights….

> The Left parties, some NGOs (and the government of India) form a third strand demanding panchayat elections under existing laws, pointing to the fact that panchayat elections have been held in Jharkhand (and Bihar) for 28 years. A fourth strand consists of Maoists who are opposed to elections, but have formed their own village assemblies to replace traditional feudal structures like headmen. (Sundar 2005, 4430)

These four strands correspond to the assertions of the Adivasi community, the non-party micro-movements, the left-subaltern vanguard, and the militant left vanguard, respectively. The OBCs and the militant left see no value in PESA, albeit for different reasons. The Adivasis and the left-subaltern NGOs are willing to engage with PESA on different rallying points, that is, customary law and elections, respectively.

Incomplete adoption of PESA in Fifth Schedule States

In my view, the incomplete adoption of PESA in all Fifth Schedule states cannot be fully grasped until we learn about the changes taking place in the tribal communities as well. What is the social-cultural profile of the leadership that is likely to be elected to the Gram Sabha? How has the leadership dynamics been impacted by development programmes? Is the leadership educated? What is their sense of tradition? What is the social stratification of the tribal social structure? How many people are landless? What is the pattern of migration? What is the record of atrocities? The fate of PESA depends on these and other related questions.

PESA became an integral part of a range of legislations for the settlement and protection of local rights to forest use. Other major legislations are:

> The Indian Forest Act 1927 (and previous 1878 Act) particularly Section 28 providing for 'village forests'; The Indian Constitution (1949), specifically Schedule V and VI providing special Constitutional protection to the resource rights of tribal communities; Ministry

of Environment and Forests guidelines of September 18, 1990 for resolving conflicts with tribal and other forest dwellers related to forest land as well as the 1988 national forest policy. (Springate-Baginski, et al. 2009, 15)

Labour Teleology and the Forest Rights Act 2006

An important reason why there were no provisions for tribal rights over land and livelihood is the absence of any record of rights of tribal people. The FRA 2006 emerged from a long struggle to correct this historic neglect (for details, see Bose 2010). A very significant aspect of labour teleology is the fact that it posits itself as an instrument for liberation. It sets itself the goal to pull human beings out of the 'state of nature', to ensure the 'retreat of the natural boundary', and 'elevate social being from any mere nature boundedness'.[3]

Political activists, political parties, civil society organisations, and a section of the State represented by the bureaucracy perceive the FRA 2006 as a milestone in the history of tribal social movements. It has won for the tribal forest people their long overdue rights over 'forest land'. On the ground, however, reports say that the process of implementation is facing several problems. At the root of these problems is the unwillingness of the Forest Department to let go of the forest land under its jurisdiction. It is clear that there is a conflict over 'forest land rights', between the Forest Department and the tribal-forest people.

Is the conflict an outcome of labour teleology? Since the enactment of FRA 2006, tribal struggles have been pressurising the State to give a handful of acres of 'forest land', as promised in this Act. Over more than 100 years, several factors have led to the material resources of the forest being removed from the material universe of the forest. What is left for tribal forest people after this reduction is a handful of acres of 'forest land'. The substance of this dilution is the taking away of the 'foundational position' of forests.

How did this domain of mother earth get eroded? It appears that the processes of labour teleology being put in place since 1773 took away from the tribal protest its insistence on a teleology-free sense of belonging to mother earth, and reduced it to accepting the view that the perceived deprivation of tribal people can be addressed by demanding from the State minimal rights to forest land.

Labour teleology worked though several avenues to undermine the foundational position of the forest. Labour teleology of the mainstream economy, driven by industrial notions of progress, of dominant cultural codes, of enlightened social sciences (history, sociology, anthropology), and of democratic left, right, and centre modes of political ideologies converged to deny tribal forest dwellers the adequate and appropriate time and space required for a teleology-free mode of being and belonging in the world. They were consequently pulled into a world shaped and structured by labour teleology. This is comparable to pulling out a tree that is firmly grounded. This process has been violent and the depth of the damages caused as yet not fathomed.

Labour teleology used liberation theology, Sanskritisation, legislations, economic development programmes, and education to distribute tribal forest dwellers over the left, right, and the centre. There was no option other than to participate in the industrial mainstream economy. The option of non-teleological modes of being was eliminated. According to this teleology, it was necessary for people to abide by the goals and means made available by the State.

Most of the forest dwellers shifted out of the forest became, over time, part of the industrial economy. What remained with them were cultural modes that had their origins in the forest, and which now had no link with the work that they did. Forest dwellers became tribal people. Today, where are the forest dwellers? They are just a handful of people living far away in the forest. This transformed the social and cultural background as also the ideological orientation of the people engaged in tribal social movements. They were subordinated to the assumptions and necessities of the State. Their frame of reference was determined by these presuppositions and necessities. In this frame, the forest is not in its foundational position because this place has been taken over by capital.

By 1996, labour teleology had served the interests of capital and had produced a large reserve army of labour. At a workshop on forest workers organised in 1996 by the National Centre for Labour in

Dehradun, their number was estimated to be between three and eight crores. B. K. Roy-Burman (1998) has listed a diversity of forest workers:

(a) Slash and burn cultivators and upland cultivators who depend on the forest primarily to sustain their traditional subsistence economy.
(b) Gatherers of non-wood forest products.
(c) Hunters fully or partly deriving their livelihood (in the form of direct consumption, local barter, and wider commercial linkage) by hunting, including trapping birds and animals whose normal habitats are in the forest.
(d) Extractors of grass, bamboo, logs, and timbers as head loads for personal use or local sales.
(e) Artisans and craftsmen dependent on forest produce.
(f) Practitioners and users of a herbal medicine system.
(g) Farmers, particularly belonging to tribal communities, whose economy is by and large a subsistence economy, which is to a considerable extent dependent on the forest ecology or changes in the forest ecology.
(h) Participants in social forestry programmes (other than recreational forestry), including the Joint Forest Management Programme (JFM), primarily for meeting basic consumption needs or for creating the social infrastructure meant especially to serve the vulnerable sections of society.
(i) Full-time or part-time wage labour employed by Forest Department Corporations, co-operatives, and ancillary bodies operating in forestry sectors as well as by contractors and lessees operating in this sector on the rights directly or indirectly obtained from the concerned forest department.
(k) Population below the poverty line (BPL) in any category of forest.

This plurality of forest workers can be arranged along a spectrum, beginning with forest dwellers and gradually moving towards forest workers who live in villages, towns, or cities. This spectrum arranges them in order of their proximity to the forest. Their material conditions for work differ accordingly. This has implications for the nature, value, and quality of work that they do. On one end of the spectrum are the forest dwellers, for whom the forest is a home and a place of work, and on the other end are people below the poverty line, who only come to work in the forest at very low wages. The forest dwellers belong to the forest, and possess the technology and the knowledge systems that enable them to dwell in and on the 'presence of the forest'. The people below the poverty line, in contrast, have neither of these; they are therefore absolutely deforested. Forest dwellers live on the frontiers. This togetherness of home and place of work created conditions that made it possible to discover the medicinal properties of plants without the theoretical and practical equipment of modern science, have a 'zero carbon footprint', and be free of debt.

How has the FRA 2006 affected the forest workers? Is the Act designed to undo over a century of injustices done to the forest dwellers and tribal people? It is important to remember that justice is appropriate and adequate only if it measures up to the depth and scale of injustice(s). With the aid of which facts did the bureaucrats, academics, planners, and political and civil society activists who applauded this Act for 'undoing historic injustices' perceive the depth and scale of these injustices?

The truth is that history shows the depth and scale of injustices and damages to be no less than genocide and ecocide. Over the past several decades, it is becoming very clear that modern sciences, especially economics, have failed to estimate the value of the damages and injustices, as well as their equivalent compensation and rehabilitation. It follows, then, that the policies and legislations that derive their legitimacy from these sciences cannot bring about justice. It is worth considering that the FRA 2006 has been legitimised by claims stating that it is in the interest of the people; however, it is in fact in the interest of the newly forged alliance between the State and the market. This is reflected in the form and content of the FRA 2006.

Land rights over a mere handful of acres are seen by social activists, academics, and NGOs working for tribal justice as undoing 100 years of injustice. This reflects the alienation of the modern environmental and ecological activist thinking from the lives of people. It has three attributes, and a close study shows that each of these attributes has determined the form and content of the FRA 2006. *First*, this thinking has been subjugated to the presuppositions and the necessity of the State. The presuppositions are that in reality, people do not have any sense of justice, that the notion of the State represents the substance of justice, viz., freedom, equality, and liberty. The dichotomy between the ideal and the real that underlies the presuppositions determines the form and content of this Act. This alienates ecological and environmental thinking from the worldview and practices of forest dwellers and tribal people.

Second, the critical component of this thinking does not see that the Act is an expression of the 'universal will' based on the notion of industrial labour as subject and nature as object. This breaks the contiguity between the work of nature and the work of man and generates private property on the one hand, and conflicts between citizenship and cultural belonging, and technology and nature, on the other. These conflicts alienate ecological and environmental thinking from the forest work processes that generate value.

Finally, its design promotes industrial capital; intensifies conflict between capital and labour; destroys the link between development and well-being; ruptures the alignment between legislation and justice; brings together violence and reason; and deforms the relation between the individual and the collective. To deal with these conflicts, the ruling class deems it necessary that the State have monopoly over instruments of violence. This alienates environmental and ecological thinking from the voices of the people.

We can now study how these attributes have determined the form and content of FRA 2006. In the FRA 2006, there is a dichotomy between the Ideal and the Real. The Preamble states,

> ... Forest rights were not adequately recognised in the consolidation of State forests during the colonial period as well in [as] independent India resulting in historical injustice to forest dwelling Scheduled Tribes and other traditional forest dwellers....
>
> ... It becomes necessary to address the longstanding insecurity of tenurial and access rights of forest dwelling Scheduled Tribes and other traditional forest dwellers including those who were forced to relocate their dwellings due to development interventions.

Thus, the FRA is 'an Act to provide for a framework for recording the forest rights so vested and the nature of evidence required for such recognition and vesting in respect of forest land' (p. 1). This, it is posited, will prepare the ground for 'sustainable use, [and] conservation of biodiversity and maintenance of ecological balance ... while ensuring livelihood and food security ...' (ibid.). In reality, however, the debate preceding this Act made it very clear that the 'rights' to 'forest land' seek to regularise 'encroachments'.

> Some opponents[4] ... claim that to distribute ... land to each adivasi nuclear family in the country ... creates fear that entire forests will then get wiped out. In reality, the bill only seeks to recognise what is already there, i.e., to give land rights to people who have been cultivating forest land for generations (before 1980), often 'reserved' without due settlement of traditional land rights. (FRA 2006, Preamble)

In fact, the entitlements to be created under the Bill are consistent with the existing policy framework, in particular the '1990 guidelines' formulated by the Ministry of Environment and Forests (and partially implemented). These guidelines put in place a procedure for the regularisation of so-called 'encroachments' that occurred prior to the cut-off date of 1980. The basic purpose of the Bill is similar, and the same cut-off date is being used (Bhatia 2005). This is in contradiction to the preamble of this Act!

How can we know the intention underlying this Act? The Act only requires the government to give legal recognition to lands that people have already been farming prior to 2005 (and, in the case of non-STs, for the past seventy-five years). Sections 3(1)(a), 4(3), and 4(6) of the Act state that people will only receive rights to 'land under their occupation' since prior to 13 December 2005, up to a ceiling of 4 hectares: that is, if I am a tribal cultivating half-an-acre of forest land as on 13 December 2005, I will receive title to exactly that half acre, and no more. If I am cultivating 10 hectares (2.5 acres) (Sanyal 2006), I receive title to 4 hectares of those; and if I am cultivating nothing, I receive title to nothing. No one will receive rights to fallow lands. Moreover, the titles recognised under this Act cannot be sold or transferred to anyone (see FRA 2006, Section 4[4]).

This, it is stated, is regularising tribal 'encroachments'. According to the Ministry of Environment and Forests, the total area of forest land under 'encroachment' (whether by Adivasi or other communities) is 13 lakh hectares. This is less than 2 per cent of the recorded forest area in the country (Bhatia 2005; Shah 2005). Approximately 88 per cent of the forest area with the State has been acquired by deception (its own encroachment is described as 'regularising tribal encroachments'). By regularising 'tribal encroachment', this Act is in fact consolidating State encroachment! How deeply does State encroachment damage the forest and injure the forest dwellers and tribal people?

The history of State encroachment will give us a clear understanding of the inhumanity of the processes of primitive accumulation of capital, its depth, and scale of the injustices and damages. Historically, the exercise of the universal will has ruptured and smashed to smithereens several modes of mutually nurturing 'shared forest time and space' that have evolved over several generations to constitute the ancestral domain. In other words, this rupture deforested the ancestral domain and undermined the diverse ways in which the universe of the forest nurtured the forest dwellers, and in turn was nurtured by them. This resulted in genocide and ecocide, which are in fact the destruction of the foundational value and position of the ancestral domain and of the forest universe, not only for the forest dwellers but also for the larger society. At the core of mutual nurturing is a sense of belonging to that (natural part of the world) which is not a product of human work.

It is on account of this mutuality that the universe of the forest is neither subject nor object. Mutuality determined both its foundational value and gave it a sense of belonging. That is to say, it is not possible to belong to a place and own it as well, because belonging comes with mutuality, which is premised on the acceptance that there is no legitimate ground for ownership of the 'right to disposal' over that which has not been created by human work.

The FRA 2006 is a Negation of Mutuality. The record of 'forest rights' is a negation of this foundational value and of belonging. It creates private property and legitimises the right to dispose of 'mutuality'. What injustice will the people suffer once 'forest rights are adequately recognised'? Will the recording of forest rights stop State encroachment? What kind of injustice is encroachment? It is a crime because it is destructive of the forest, which is of intrinsic foundational value to the forest dwellers. The criminological question, in other words, is not so much how some people come to have an attitude of moral indifference or aggression towards other human beings, as much as why some people feel free to act destructively towards the material world to which other people attach great intrinsic value.[5]

How does this struggle that went into the making of the FRA 2006 compare with the struggle Birsa Munda undertook? Birsa Munda struggled for the ancestral domain and not for 'forest land rights'. Compared to Birsa Munda's perception, the FRA 2006 is a colossal dilution of the struggle. How did this happen? This brings us to the second attribute, the break in the contiguity between the work of nature and the work of human beings.

The provision for 'Critical wildlife habitats' (hereafter CWLH) (FRA 2006, Ch. III 4, 2) ensures this break. It is stated that

> the forest rights recognized under the Act in critical wildlife habitats of national parks and sanctuaries may subsequently be modified and resettled, provided that no forest rights holders shall be resettled or have their rights in any manner affected for the purpose of creating inviolate areas for wildlife conservation.... (p. 168, this volume)

This implies that 'forest land' is recognised even within a CWLH, and 'relocation is possible only when it is established that coexistence is not possible and if the local communities give their informed consent'.

With this Act, the debate between 'tigers vs. tribals' has been intensified. Will the rights to 'forest land' in and around CWLH threaten the tiger and biodiversity? This Act put in place conditions that will make such coexistence impossible. Is the coexistence of the tiger and tribal people a viable proposition in present-day conditions of economy? There are still several places where forest dwellers and wildlife coexist. These forest dwellers are on the frontiers, because they have a zero carbon footprint and their lives are, relatively speaking, free of debts. The threat to coexistence comes from external forces—the 'rights regime' and the construction of 'reserves of nature'.

For instance, in order to fully appreciate the logic underlying the construction of reserves of nature (national parks, sanctuaries, and biosphere reserves), it is necessary to ask: Has introducing a break in the contiguity between the work of nature and the work of human beings been effective for conservation? A related question is: What is the intention underlying the making of these 'reserves'?

The tussle between the tribals and the tiger is in fact a non-issue. That it has become important is because of a political economy associated with these 'reserves of nature'. Without mutual nurturing, both human beings and wildlife are threats to each other; this is what we learn from the life of the forest dwellers. Dwelling makes this mutuality possible. Dwelling is to be at home, to belong to a place by contemplation on where (time, place, and space) one belongs. To be at home involves reciprocity—the inhabitants of the forest also need to be comfortable with human beings.

Viewed from the perspective of forest dwellers, the construction of nature reserves is a violation of this mutuality. From the standpoint of environmentalists who defend the tiger, the tribals are encroachers who have been largely responsible for deforestation, especially through their practices of shifting cultivation and hunting. This view has been critiqued time and again. History records the reckless logging by the Forest Department and timber mafia, mining, and industries as the key 'criminal acts' in this regard. Further, there is no evidence to show that the State forest bureaucracy manages reserves of nature better than the tribal forest dweller. The current 'reserves of nature' regime is largely responsible for poaching. It is equally responsible for generating conflicts between different government departments, thereby putting conservation in jeopardy.

The tiger is in the centre, supported by the State because it is the totem of masculinity, of power, of the accompanying macho public culture of conquest. It also stands for the patriarchal mode of looking at 'natural resources as capital'. A defence of the tiger carries forward the tradition of destroying all that is feminine in nature and culture, and legitimises the political ecology of the surplus value, capital, and the industrial system. This tradition has been well-documented by Carolyn Merchant in her book, *The Death of Nature* (1980).

The 'death of nature' refers to the destruction of labor as a gendered mode of being in the world. By themselves, the feminine elements do not constitute the culture of 'care', 'nurture', and sharing. This culture requires masculine elements as well. In the gendered mode of being, the masculine and the feminine together shape the relation of human beings to nature. With the death of nature, the 'forest dwellings' were transformed into 'reserves of nature'. This change was a consequence of 'industrial labour positing' that these 'reserves' were an integral component of the instrumentations developed by liberal economic regimes for the survival of life on earth, which was under threat on account of the environment crisis. As we all know, this crisis was a result of the reckless industrial growth which had consumed its resource base without ensuring their renewal, and jeopardised not just itself, but life on earth as well.

This is a clear demonstration of how capital ensures its immortality by first positing that the environmental crisis threatens the world, and then subsequently positioning itself as the only means available to resolve the crisis.

The 1972 UN Conference on the Human Environment at Stockholm, the 1973 European Communities Club of Rome Conference, the 1992 Rio Declaration at Rio de Janeiro, Brazil, the 1997 Kyoto Earth Summit on Global Warming have all determined three elements emerging from this crisis: speed, conservation, and sustainability. With these elements, capital reproduction is further ensured.

The speed of industrial production and reproduction is several times greater than the speed at which nature can regenerate the resources required for sustaining this system. It is this speed that underlies deforestation, the loss of biodiversity, pollution, drying up of rivers and groundwater resources, the expanding hole in the ozone layer, the rise in temperature by 2 degrees centigrade, etc. In such a situation, sustainability as we know it today is not concerned with the possibility of slowing down. Conservation is concerned with the question: How can this economy be made sustainable at this speed and without any further destruction of natural resources?

Capital investment in conservation and renewable energy systems is recommended as the way to do this. It is expected that these reserves of nature will become instruments of conservation that will contain further destruction and also provide biotic materials at a pace that is in keeping with industrial production. It is for this reason that ex-situ and in-situ conservation are related. Ethno-botanists extract resources from forests, which are conserved as reserves of nature (ex-situ), and biotic materials—germ plasmas, and genetic materials—are preserved in the laboratory (in-situ). Without this arrangement, two life-supporting industries, namely agro-food and pharmaceuticals, will be in crisis.

Conservation is not concerned with finding ways to slow down. Why is slowing down not a possibility and why can conservation not actively engage forest workers?

The principle 'labour as subject and nature as object' is embedded in the definitions of forest rights (Chapters II and III of the FRA 2006). The creation of a reserve of nature contributes to the making of a reserve army of labour. The speed of industrial production is also the speed at which capital reproduces itself. This determines the rate of technological innovation which, in direct proportion, determines the speed of extraction of natural resources on the one hand and the formation of the reserve army of labour on the other.

The provisions in Chapters II and III of the FRA 2006 lay down procedures that will lead to the creation of a reserve army of labour. These chapters describe two kinds of forest rights, namely individual family rights and community rights. Both do not allow for any kind of co-existence between non-human nature and human beings. Individual rights over not more than 4 hectares of 'forest land' are inalienable. A nuclear family can acquire this right over 'forest land' that has been used within a period of twenty-five years, from 1980 to 2005. Evidence of use will have to be submitted by the claimant through the Gram Sabha and verified by the government. This is expected to fulfil their needs for habitation and livelihood through self-cultivation.

There is a long way to go before all rights are settled. What is the intention underlying these provisions? Were there considerations other than to address injustices that contributed to the making of this Act? What role did the larger context have in the making of this Act? Under no circumstances will 4 hectares be sufficient for subsistence and survival. We do not know the quality of those 4 hectares; how was 4 hectares decided upon in the first place? When, over two generations, the nuclear family grows in size, 4 hectares will become insufficient. Why is the registration of rights in the name of both spouses and not in the name of women?

In the light of past experience, it would not be incorrect to say that forest dwellers will have to look for work outside their 'forest land'. In other words, all of them are likely to become part of the reserve army of labour, and women will continue to be subjected to patriarchal regimes. It is clear that the restriction of forest land rights to 4 hectares is a 'land ceiling' for the poor sections of a village community, largely the landless people. Community rights are with respect to water bodies, grazing lands, habitats, pastoral lands, etc. This is expected to fulfil their needs for minor forest produce, fish, cattle products, etc.

However, the Act does not say how many hectares would come under community rights. Is a community made up only of people who have 4 hectares of forest land, or does it comprise the entire village community? Who will decide the principles of sharing? Are rights to nuclear families likely to contribute to the making of communities, or are they going to further fragment village social life? The play of power structures will depend on the population composition, the land distribution, and stratification of a village.

In Mendha Lekha, a village in District Gadchiroli, Maharashtra, people took the initiative to look after their ancestral forest much before the Act came into being. This Act was used by them to strengthen the relation between individual and community rights. However, where there is no people's movement and where the ratio of the tribal to the non-tribal population is in favour of the former, the fragmentation process is likely to deepen. Between these two lies a whole range of situations. The dialectics between these two sets of rights will only emerge as the process of settlement of rights unfolds.

Does not the FRA 2006 prepare the ground for Carbon Colonialism? The category 'forest land' is embedded in the notion of industrial labour and is a result of the 'secularisation' of labour, which takes away all its transcendental elements. This is at the core of industrial capital and labour relations.

In principle, 'forest land' is derived from two different fields, namely the universe of the forest and land. The forest is three-dimensional on account of the height (the third dimension) of the canopy provided by the trees, and in contrast, the plain surface of land is two-dimensional. The forest is a universe between the earth and the sky. According to forest dwellers, the meeting of the earth and the sky is a sure sign of disaster. They should, therefore, never meet, and this is why the presence of the trees is necessary. This forms the transcendental element—the third dimension—which is introduced by the trees, and is a significant aspect of foundational value. The presence of trees builds resilience and their absence enhances vulnerability.

The intrinsic value of the forest universe is thus derived from the canopy. The canopy shelters. The intertwining diversity of the space-time continuum creates clearings for care and nurture. Clearings are camouflaged niche dwellings, invigorated by the play of heat, light, and shadow, the sun and the moon, by the togetherness of the masculine and the feminine. Here, human settlements and wildlife co-exist, mutually sheltering. In contrast, 'land' is without canopy. It is a flat surface that extends to the horizon. There is no intertwining continuum, no clearing, and no camouflages. The making of the horizon is the first step in the secularisation of labour. It is for this reason that there is no possibility of the co-existence of human settlements with wildlife.

The category 'forest land' disconnects the trees from the universe of the forest. What happens to the trees when they are disconnected from this universe? The tree is stripped of its transcendental elements and is viewed in terms of the services it can provide, which have been termed 'ecological services'. In other words, 'forest land' is designed for ecological services. Embedded in the notion of 'forest land' is a change in the perception of the forest and forestry.

From this perspective, community forestry is being developed to create carbon sinks. In October 2001, Community Forestry International (CFI) published a report exploring how payments for carbon capture could be made to rural communities in Madhya Pradesh, in return for their successful regeneration of degraded teak forests. As the mechanisms to channel environmental service payments to community resource managers are still in an early phase of development, this is a landmark study. The report explores the feasibility of using carbon credit-based financing mechanisms to support community forest restoration initiatives in India. Participating in the study were scientists from the Indian Institute of Forests, Bhopal and the Centre for Ecological Sciences (CES) at the Indian Institute of Science (IISc), Bangalore. Funding for the project was provided by the USDA Forest Service, Office of International Programs, and the USAID Global Bureau.

In November 2002, CFI published a second report titled, 'The Clean Development Mechanism and Village-Based Forest Restoration: A Case Study from Adilabad District, Andhra Pradesh, India' (Poffenberger, et al. 2002). The report describes cost-effective methods for assessing carbon additionality, developed by the CES at IISc, Bangalore. In central India, the Gond tribal Forest Protection Committees (FPC), referred to as the Vana Samarakshana Samithi (VSS), and self-help groups (SHGs) are already involved in managing watershed restoration contracts and enrichment planting of valuable trees, such as the Indian beech (*pongamia pinnata*) and jatropha. This strategy has multiple advantages in terms of creating terrestrial carbon sinks, providing bio-diesel fuels as an alternative to fossil fuels and thereby offsetting carbon emissions, and re-establishing the hydrological functions of degraded watersheds.[6]

There is increasing support for involving tribal forest dweller communities in regimes providing forest services. Forest planners and forest departments are being persuaded to not ignore the local ecological services provided by forests, and to recognise that the forest community's knowledge can contribute to these services (Kumar 2001).

The environment minister stated:

> The State budget for forests shall remain unaffected and the fund being transferred would be in addition to State Budget and it is expected that all States will utilize this fund towards forestry activities to achieve the objectives of the Nationally-Determined Contributions (NDCs) of increasing its forest & tree cover, which will create an additional carbon sink equivalent to 2.5 to 3 billion tonnes of carbon dioxide by the year 2030. (Ministry of Environment, Forest and Climate Change 2019)

However, who are the carbon sinks for? It is well-known that the emissions of greenhouse gases that are creating problems come overwhelmingly from the richer industrialised countries that do have the resources to adapt. For example, the USA and the EU, with only 10 per cent of the world's population, are responsible for producing 45 per cent of all emissions of carbon dioxide (CO2), the principal greenhouse gas. Carbon-fixing is the new instrument known as CO2lonialism (see Eraker 2000). In particular, this trend can be seen in the use of monoculture plantations, which allegedly 'sequester' or remove CO2 from the atmosphere. Therefore, there is no scientific credibility to the practice of soaking up pollution using tree plantations (Bachram 2004). This is because unlike oil, natural gas, and coal, the carbon dioxide reserved in trees and other biomass is very unstable as it may be released back into the atmosphere at any time through burning and logging. Yet the State in India is looking towards entrepreneurial companies for the use of community forestry in carbon consumption (Nozaki 2023).

The positing of labour teleology seems to have no foresight. It cannot look beyond what it posits, which is rapid profits, capital accumulation, and the production of a reserve army of labour on the one hand, and deep ecological crisis on the other. It is unable to see that every effort being made to deal with this crisis is integral to the cycle of capital accumulation. Capital establishes its immortality and invincibility. It produces and reproduces complex cycles of the production and reproduction of violence at all levels of social existence.

What lies beyond the labour teleology? What can we learn from the struggles that are being undertaken to ensure the implementation of the FRA 2006? The struggle needs to go beyond this implementation and decommission labour teleology as well as reach out to the foundational position of the universe of the forest.

Can labour teleology of positing be decommissioned? This question is premised on the understanding that the nature and scope of labour cannot be restricted to goals posited for it to achieve. According to Charles S. Peirce, goals are 'nothing but "operative desires", the objects of which are never concrete, but always general'. From this perspective, does not the production and acquiring these desired objects constitute only one aspect of labour? Can decommissioning this aspect of labour facilitate the teleological unfolding of labor as a mode of discovering the self and the world it inhabits?

Endnotes

1. These talks were initiated in the 1980s, jointly by the USA, the European Union, and Japan, to promote free trade and economic globalisation.

2. Thungon to consider Constitutional Amendment. On 15 May 1989 the Constitution (64th Amendment) Bill was introduced in Parliament. See http://indiansaga.com/history/postindependence/institutions2.html (accessed June 2023).

3. Each of these expressions are used by Rousseau, Marx, and Lukacs, respectively.

4. The opponent referred to here is the Forest Department.

5. Both the looting of antiquities and the destruction of forests involve damage to insentient objects which are highly valued by some people, in ways not reducible to economic value. Such crimes (and the question whether they should be labelled as crimes at all) pose a challenge to those forms of critical criminology, or studies of social harm, which look beyond legal definitions of crime and seek to ground their approach in some kind of sociology of morality. Damage to objects or plants does not fit easily either into a human rights based approach.

> The criminological question, in other words, is not so much how some people come to have an attitude of moral indifference or aggression towards other human beings (Pemberton, 2004), but why some people feel free to act destructively towards features of the material world to which other people attach great intrinsic value. What would appear to be lacking or neutralized in such cases is not (or not only) empathy, but some other kind of moral emotion or evaluative attitude. To identify what this is involves an investigation of the phenomenology of value.' (Ward 2009)

6. See www.communityforestryinternational.org (accessed May 2023).

four

Labo(u)ring with Language*

This chapter discusses the language of instrumental labour underlying the legislations discussed in Chapter Three and draws attention to the labo(u)r potential in relation to three categories: 'Scheduled Tribe', 'Indigenous', and 'Adivasi'.

It is argued that the different value assigned to the language of the people determines labo(u)r potential. This is based on the understanding that language can bring forth the possibilities embedded in labo(u)r power as well as destroy it. For instance, the labour potential is destroyed when the labour power of an able body is deprived of the nourishment of language. The history of the primitive accumulation of capital, which extends from feudalism to contemporary neoliberalism (Perelman 2007; von Werlhof 2000), shows that the state of nature designated by the category 'able body' legitimises two interrelated attributes of primitive accumulation. First, the necessary use of force to divorce the producer from the means of production.[1] Language is one such means of production. Second, a total disregard for the significance of landscape nature, the lives of the people, and their rules, laws, customs, and practices (prevalent particularly in places outside Europe; see Luxemburg 1951, Ch. 27). History has shown that the forces of revolution, war, and oppressive taxation have been used to pull people out of the 'state of nature'.

*An earlier version of this chapter was published as 'Primitive Accumulation and Labor and the Making of "Scheduled Tribe", "Indigenous", and "Adivasi Sensibility"', in Meena Radhakrishna (ed.), *First Citizens-Studies on Adivasis, Tribals, and Indigenous Peoples in India*. New Delhi: Oxford University Press, 2016.

The category 'Scheduled Tribe' was created historically as a part of the process of primitive accumulation by totally disregarding the language and landscapes of the forest dwellers, in order to bring them into the realm of mainstream labour. The category 'indigenous' historically emerged to resist these aspects of primitive accumulation as a necessary step to realise the labor potential. The category 'Adivasi' historically presented itself to give expression to a sensibility that is not determined by the processes of primitive accumulation; in other words, it says 'no' to this process. In this lies the possibility of realising labour potentiality.

'Scheduled Tribes': Denial of Language as Counter-Insurgency

The category 'Scheduled Tribes' (ST) was created in 1950 by the Indian Constituent Assembly. It carried forward the colonial determination to counter insurgencies against primitive accumulation, pull insurgent forest dwellers and peasants out of natural landscape economies, and bring them within the folds of the irreversible universal labour-time of social production and reproduction of capital.

The British colonial rulers constructed a forestry regime for primitive accumulation. This regime was legitimised by Adam Smith's argument in his *History of British India*, which states that under primitive conditions, land belongs to the sovereign. Rosa Luxemburg pointed out that this argument was based on dubious historical evidence and distortions of practices in India (Luxemburg 1951, 352, 353, fn1). It determined the directive principle of primitive accumulation that legitimised the territorial sovereignty of the State, namely that all land, unknown or known, used or unused belongs to the State, and land that does not give revenue is wasteland (Baden-Powell 1974 [1892], Vol. 2, 379). The teleology of this directive was to convert all wasteland into revenue land. Thus, all the forest and land used by forest dwellers and peasants for their livelihood was classified as 'wasteland' because it did not generate revenue.

This legitimised, in the period between the mid-eighteenth and mid-nineteenth century (between 1760 and 1860), an aggressive primitive accumulation by commercial forestry and large-scale single-crop commercial agriculture. Richard Grove (1995, 386–392) points out that under the East India Company regime in the 1760s, there was timber shortage because of the reckless extraction to provide for the construction of railway tracks, development of the ship-building industry, making furniture, and ensuring a continuous supply of firewood. Between 1760 and 1790 in both Bengal and Bombay Presidencies, this led the Company to expand its territory to gain resources from areas inhabited by forest dwellers and peasants. This was the beginning of forestry in irreversible linear time, because the extraction of timber was determined by commercial demand. The Permanent Settlement of 1793 also initiated large-scale commercial agriculture.

The commercial necessity to meet the demands gave legitimacy to the idea of conservation of forest resources and prepared the ground for the creation of 'reserves of nature'. This economic necessity for conservation was at the basis of the Dalhousie Memorandum of 1855, which led to a centralised forest-management policy, adopted in India after 1860 (Grove 1995, 460–461). The institutional set-up to conserve forests for commerce was inaugurated in 1864, when Dietrich Brandis was appointed as the first Inspector General of Forest to the Government of India. In that year, the Forest Department of Bengal was set up and a Conservator of Forest recruited. This idea and institution were legitimised by the first Indian Forest Act of 1865. It was modified in 1873–1874 and in 1878, and in 1924, a new Forest Act was implemented, replacing the previous one (of 1865) (Ghosal 2011, 111).

This forestry regime undertook the expansion of forest territory after 1800 (Grove 1995, 390) to include remote areas as 'reserves of nature', because commercial use was not possible without forcibly taking away the forest and land from the tribal forest dwellers and peasants, which was their means of production. During these years of expansion, there were at least 110 known instances of insurgency over a period of 117 years, from 1783–1900 (Guha 1983, 13). Shachi

Arya (1998, 216–220) has chronologically recorded the history of insurgency from 1778 onwards.

No effort was made to listen to what the people were trying to say. Their language was disregarded. This was integral to the labour teleology underlying the primitive accumulation of capital. In 'Elementary Structures' the 'language of the people' is what the counter-insurgency lens selected. The language of the people is certainly more than what this lens focuses on. This legitimised measures to counter the insurgencies, get timber without difficulty, and more importantly, to pull forest dwellers and peasants out of the 'state of nature'. Warren Hastings' Cultural Policy of 1773 and the Queen's Proclamation of 1858 prepared the ground for constructing appropriate counter-insurgency measures in accordance with this teleology. The cultural policy advocated an informed culturally sensitive governance. The Queen's Proclamation declared a policy of non-interference with language and culture.

> ...We declare it Our royal will and pleasure that .... none be molested or disquieted, by reason of their religious faith or observances, but that all shall alike enjoy the equal and impartial protection of the law; and We do strictly charge and enjoin all those who may be in authority under Us that they abstain from all interference with the religious belief or worship of any of Our subjects on pain of Our highest displeasure..... (Belmekki 2008, 117)

This Proclamation did not negate the cultural policy, but suggested 'non-interference' as the frame through which to know and understand the social and cultural life of the people. To 'abstain from all interference' legitimised administrative arrangements for documenting social and cultural practices and for taking away from forest dwellers and peasants their means of subsistence—land and forest. In other words, the importance of the language of practices for their means of subsistence was disregarded.

On the one hand, the areas inhabited by un-reconciled forest people were maintained under military control and were known as non-regulated areas. In other areas, known as 'Regulation Districts', civilians were employed to look after the administration. In these districts, the ancient rights of people were recognised by the Scheduled

Districts Act of 1874 and 'The Agency Tracts, Interest, and Land Transfer Act of 1917'. On the other hand, these Acts protected limited rights to use forest materials for subsistence by declaring them as inalienable and non-transferable.

With the construction of the categories 'restricted' and 'unrestricted', insurgents were suppressed and co-opted. Suppression clamped down on the forest time and space that formed the basis of ancient (customary) rights, and co-option brought them into the frame of linear irreversible productive time. Both are now integral to postcolonial governance and have become part of a modern worldview. On the other hand, as part of the exercise to understand the culture of people, the Census of India 1931 used the two categories of 'caste' and 'tribe' to divide insurgents. These categories were created through ethnological inquiries of India, under the direction of J. H. Hutton, by the Cambridge anthropologist-administrators who had served the colonial State. Soon after, under the Government of India Act of 1935, the unrestricted and restricted areas became excluded and partially excluded areas.

In 1950, the Constitution of independent India designated these areas as the Fifth and Sixth Scheduled Areas. The 73rd Amendment to the Constitution in 1992, PESA 1996, the carving out of new tribal states—Chattisgarh and Jharkhand—in 2000, and the FRA 2006 have not undone this structure; for instance, in these legislations, the recognition of customary rights is a continuation of the 'recognition of ancient rights' by the Queen's Proclamation of 1858, and not its critique.

Contemporary legal regimes continue to pull tribal people out of the 'state of nature' and bring both them and nature within the folds of the non-cyclical linear time of production and reproduction of commodities and capital accumulation. Are the struggles to implement PESA and the FRA against the neoliberal programmes for economic development? Are these Acts not instruments to counter insurgency and facilitate primitive accumulation of neoliberal capital? The teleology of land and forest revenue legislation underlying these Acts is directed by capital's struggle against 'natural economy' and the 'state of nature'.

The category 'Scheduled Tribe' now has four counter-insurgency functions: political, economic, security, and information. Its political function is to ensure the reconciliation with and reform of governance. Its economic function is to provide essential services and stimulate long-term economic growth, build confidence in the government, and reduce the level of frustration amongst the landless and the unemployed youth. Its security function is to develop legal frames, civilian oversight mechanisms, and judicial systems. Its information function is to bring on record the essential information about the condition of people that is necessary for governance. The legal regimes of this category also determine the postcolonial politics of recognition and development (Kapila 2008). It lays down who can be considered a tribal, eligible to be included in this category, and determines the notion of identity that is to be the basis of this recognition. Any claim to a Scheduled Tribe status today is measured against the following criteria: cultural or social identity; demarcated occupation and use of primitive technology; lack of relationship to the majority community (isolation); practice of marriage payments; practice of animist or totemic religions; and practice of endogamy. It is necessary to reflect on why there has been no discussion on these criteria. What implication does this have on people's self-perception?

Today, counter-insurgency measures continue to determine the dynamics of State power and cultural classifications. An important aspect of these measures is that they discourage any discussion on the validity of these criteria, and thus freeze 'identity'. This prepares the ground for the unfolding of an industrial labour teleology; while on the one hand there is a constitutional right to the customary practices of livelihood (granted by PESA 1996 and FRA 2006), on the other hand, according to the criteria determining a tribe, they are backward and primitive, and situated on the margins.

This absurd juxtaposition of progressive and backward elements frames the ontology of labour. The present of these people is determined by annihilating the past, and their being in a 'state of nature'. Thus, there is no value given to the labour of the ancestors of the people who have included themselves, and who have the desire to be included, in the category 'Scheduled Tribes'. The historical sense of the people under this category strives to preserve traces of what they have lost. The people's sense of their presence in the world today, in relation to other communities and to the State, is embedded in past labour, which for them is not in the 'state of nature'.

Efforts have been made to bring this sense into a constructive relation with labour, which has not happened. When the historical sense of the people starts to assert itself, the teleology of primitive accumulation works to immediately suppress it. For instance, the provisions of PESA 1996 and FRA 2006 has deprived them of the time and space necessary for traditional practices. For instance, with regard to the land and forest available under these Acts, it is not possible to conserve the diversity of the forest through the use of customary practices such as shifting cultivation. It is important to see that while these Acts pretend to empower the people, they in fact empower the State even more. It is equally important to see that the people who have benefited from being categorised as 'Scheduled Tribe' have progressively lost touch with the forest—only a few perhaps are willing to live in or around the forest. They have internalised the State view, that is, to give the forest a foundational position in their worldview is equivalent to wanting to let people stay in isolation, underdeveloped and deprived of the benefits of modern development.

The making of these Acts may at best be legislative victories, but they are in fact instances of political set-back because they have undermined people's language in the same way that tribal education institutions have. The discussion is no longer about the value of the forest, the forest worldview, its traditions, and the customary practices of caring for nature. Only a handful of people are well-versed with these. The handful of acres of land made available by these Acts (PESA and FRA 2006) has prepared the ground for a mass migration of people in the third—if not the second—generation. The forest has been displaced from its foundational position in the worldview of the people; it is no longer a living space.

This process is embedded in the understanding that, so long as labour and economy are in the 'state of nature', they cannot have exchange value. The teleology of this exchange value is to counter insurgency, pull people out of a 'state of nature', and 'civilise' them. This corrodes their labor potential.

'Indigenous' Perspective and Labor Aterity

The International Labor Organization (ILO) was the first to use the term 'indigenous' officially. Over time, an indigenous perspective has evolved against primitive accumulation.

The colonisation of what is now the United States and Canada dates back to 1492. Here, primitive accumulation by means of the law and the gun took the form of the genocide of a substantial population, of approximately as many as seven million people who had settled on these continents. This population was diverse in culture, economy, and social organisation. There were twelve distinct language groups, each embracing numerous individual tribes with differing economies—some depended on hunting game and gathering food from the forests and meadows; others cultivated maize, beans, squash, melons, and tobacco. Efforts to dispense justice and address the suffering of the people of these continents were made only after World War I. In the Treaty of Versailles, the creation of the ILO was suggested as a measure to ensure the protection of workers. The ILO was born in 1919 and one of its first studies was concerned with indigenous workers. In 1926, the Governing Body created a Committee of Experts on native workers.

The social ethos made it necessary to initiate steps globally to combat the injurious effects of industrialisation, as an important precondition for peace was ensuring social justice for all workers. These effects resulted from an integration with and assimilation into the mainstream. The key terms for the mainstream discourse were: nation-building, equity, development, and diversification of industrial production. Productivity was the most important determinant of this discourse, and it shaped the relation between land, labour, and capital. The technology mediating productivity, equity, and development was based on the binary of modernity and tradition. The most significant aspect of this discourse was that people's social and cultural traditions of work (which linked their knowledge systems to their ways of life) were considered obstacles and marginalised, since cultural perceptions of productivity differed from those of industrial production. These people were seen as being at a less advanced stage of development, largely because their social life was regulated wholly or partially by their own customs or traditions, and not by rational thinking.

In 1957, the ILO adopted Convention 107—the first treaty dealing with indigenous and tribal populations. This convention included not only aboriginal people who predated settlement or conquest, but also tribal or semi-tribal groups, irrespective of whether or not they could be regarded as indigenous in this sense (of being the first inhabitants). It included people from America, Australia, the Near and the Middle East, and from the African continent (Barsh 1986; Savyasaachi 2004; Yupsanis 2010).

With the emergence of the human rights movement during the 1970s, social and cultural factors became important for industrial production and development. It was argued that culture mediates technology and labour. The culture of the workplace was defined not only by technology alone, but also by the social and cultural background of labour; the attitudes and dispositions of labour could not be understood without taking into account people's social and cultural practices. It was clear that the social and cultural perceptions of work and of worker identity determined the social dynamics of the production process and of the workplace. Thus, the social and cultural framework for production became important. The social and cultural integration of a large mass of marginalised wage labour became an important component of the process of nation-building.

A major change occurred in 1981 with the UNESCO Declaration on Ethnocide and Ethno-development. The efforts for reconstruction post-World Wars I and II played an important role in the formulation and acceptance of this declaration. On the one hand, the UN inherited a series of political instruments signed after the Wars. These contained special measures for the protection of ethnic, religious, and linguistic groups, and referred to minorities in Poland, Austria, the Serbo–Croat–Slovenic State, Czechoslovakia, Bulgaria, Romania, Hungary, Albania, Lithuania, Greece, Turkey, Estonia, and Iraq, amongst others. On the other hand, the sordid story of Nazi genocide made it amply clear that all genocide begins with cultural aggression. From the making of this 'declaration', it was clear that a fundamental component of modernisation and development was intolerance of social-cultural diversity in its external as well as internal environment.

From this emerged the indigenous perspective that the ground for alternative development lies in pluralism, and this ground cannot be prepared without including the indigenous people, not only because they were the first to suffer, and point towards the intolerance and violence inherent in the culture of modern man, but also because they in fact constitute this plurality.

During the 1980s, indigenous peoples all over the world were engaged in struggles against invasions and genocide, militarisation, the formation of nuclear States, mining, large dams, reckless commercial forestry, pollution, missionaries, modern education, racism, exploitation of labour, forcible sterilisation of women, prison, tourism, and the forced sale of land (Moody 1988). Towards the end of the twentieth century, these struggles have multiplied and articulate a standpoint. These have enriched the indigenous perspective. From the late 1980s onwards, environment and ecology became important factors of production. Technology and finance were directed towards the preservation and conservation of the environment and ecology. Control over natural resources gradually became 'monopolistic', denying access to the people. This added to subsistence problems and brought about further marginalisation. The indigenous people were concerned with finding an alternative to this 'mainstream' way of being part of the world order and of acquiring a sense of belonging. These struggles highlighted that in addition to genocide, ecocide was also at the foundation of modernisation and development.

These understandings cleared the ground for indigenous struggles to assert in the political arena that their cultural perception of their origins lies at the basis of their sense of history. It cleared the ambiguity created by the use of several terms to refer to indigenous people: natives, aboriginal, autochthonous, ethnic minorities, tribal people, first nation, and fourth world. 'The most undisputed criterion is that indigenous peoples are the descendants of the original inhabitants of a territory taken over through conquest or settlement by aliens' (Khan and bin Talal 1987, 6). To capture the sense of 'being original inhabitants', Roger Moody (1988) used the expression 'species of origin', and suggested that their struggles are concerned with 'conscientisation and the recovery of origins'. For indigenous people, history has its origins in dispossession. In the light of 'being dispossessed', the meaning of 'species of origin' and 'recovery of origins' is defined by the substantive concerns of their contemporary struggles. For indigenous peoples, 'origins' are not dated; they cannot be determined in a frame of linear time. Origins articulate a sense of belonging that sees in landscapes the passage of time that shows the presence of larger life processes that create the potential for labo(u)r.

This changed the frame of reference. The process of industrial modernisation was no longer conceptualised in terms of the opposition between the traditional and the modern. In its place, the discourse was of the opposition between the marginalised and the dominant forces. The dominant forces monopolised the definitions, standards, and norms of social and economic life by taking control of the terms and categories of cultural and intellectual discourses. Consequently, people's sense of their own identity, their capability, and their confidence was undermined.

Against the background of all these struggles, in 1989 Convention 107 was criticised for emphasising integration and assimilation, and a revised version of this Convention was formulated, as Convention 169. This Convention stipulated that 'self-identification as indigenous or tribal shall be regarded as [the] fundamental criterion for determining the groups to which the provisions of this Convention apply'. This drew attention primarily to the endogenous efflorescence of human potential. In turn, this allowed for the definition of 'indigenous' in a historical-axiological sense and not in a purely chronological sense. The emphasis was on a plurality of relations between social formations and a sense of identity. This allowed for the inclusion of tribal people from all countries in Asia and Africa, while the purely chronological criteria applied to North and South America and Australia.

By the beginning of the 1990s, the ground had been prepared for pursuing the question of alternatives in a pluralist framework. The suffering showed that the processes of mainstream industrial modernisation had continuously unleashed social forces that had undermined the support systems that sustain life itself.

By a consensus, the Economic and Social Council (ECOSOC) established the UN Permanent Forum on Indigenous Issues on 28 July 2000, at its forty-fifth plenary meeting. Its mandate was to discuss and advise on indigenous issues relating to economic and social development, culture, the environment, education, health, and human rights within the Council on the one hand, and promote the integration and coordination of activities relating to indigenous issues within the United Nations system on the other. However, 'The Permanent Forum is not specifically given any mandate to set new standards in international law' (Khosravi Lile 2006).

In 2005, Filipino international indigenous activist Victoria Tauli Corpuz was unanimously elected Chair of the UN Permanent Forum on Indigenous Issues. In 2006, with the publication of *Paradigm Wars* (Mander and Tauli-Corpuz 2006), it was clear that the process of primitive accumulation was continuing unabated, with greater force even, and that it was being met with an equally strong resistance from indigenous people across the world.

> NO COMMUNITIES OF PEOPLES ON THIS EARTH have been more negatively impacted by the current global economic system than the world's remaining 350 million indigenous peoples. And no peoples are so strenuously and, lately, successfully resisting these invasions and inroads.
>
> It is the first purpose of this book to describe the nature, breadth and ferocity of the assaults upon native societies that are ongoing today, and the global institutions and corporations that drive them, while desperately seeking access to their own lifeblood—the planet's fast disappearing resource supply.
>
> But it is also our purpose to convey the impressive energy, scale, and clarity of purpose of a global indigenous resistance. It is growing increasingly broad, powerful, well organized, and effective in both domestic and international contexts. Indigenous peoples are demanding respect, recognition and codification of their 'prior rights' to live where they have always lived, in the manner they choose, and with control over all decisions about their ancestral lands, and what is on them and in them. (ibid., 3)

In an article in this book, Tauli Corpuz argues that traditional economic practices are the basis for the 'Right to Remain Separate and Distinct'. The traditional practices she points out are in conflict with economic globalisation, and for this reason, were labelled obstacles to progress. This 'progress' depends upon the destruction of peoples' lands and resources, and even of the genetic materials of human beings and plants. She goes into a detailed discussion of how these assaults play out through global bureaucracies, and what is being done to reverse this trend. As the species of origin, the indigenous people share a view of work, nature, and productivity that is differently institutionalised in different communities, allowing for plural work cultures. This contributed to the further enrichment of the indigenous perspective. The contours of this perspective are as follows.

According to the 'indigenous' perspective, the politics of alterity embedded in the teleology of industrial labour is manifest as genocide. Here, labour was determined in alterity to nature. Its difference from earlier genocides was two-fold. On the one hand, it is based on the view that people's cultural values determined laziness, rendering them incapable of the labour necessary for the accumulation of capital, and therefore has to be exterminated.[2] On the other hand, it prepared the ground for the emergence of a European subjectivity[3] unsettled by the imperatives of capitalist penetration. This particular subjectivity mapped the 'Other', not only in the outside world (Africa, America, etc.), but also internally in Europe and its neighbourhoods (for instance, the Jews in Germany).

The indigenous perspective argues for a relationship between technology, culture, the environment, ecology, human rights, productivity, equity, and work culture that is directed to recover and restore ecological balances, arrest environmental destruction, and prepare the ground to enrich the productive capacities of labour and prevent any violation of the right to means of subsistence. It emphasises that land, water, and forests are shared, and this is a pre-condition for security and certitude. It upholds democratic spaces where plural production norms are grounded in plural perceptions of work, nature, and productivity. Further, it holds that life-support systems can be enriched when an economy ensures plural livelihoods to all. Decentralised social organisation ensures human rights and equity, taking into account people's social and cultural traditions and practices. The history of marginalised peoples suggests that different and new methodologies be acquired to create plural livelihoods.

With this perspective, the ground is being prepared for a fresh constitution that embraces the meaning of enlightened beings in the world, one that is caring, secure, and certain of continuities in the life-world. The transition from the twentieth to the twenty-first century has been from being and living 'off the world' to being and living 'for the world'. The 'being off the world' emerges from the destructive process of globalisation, while 'being for the world' emerges from care for the life-world. Life-support systems for 'being off the world' are discontinuous with the production system. In 'being for the world', however, production and reproduction systems are contiguous with the life-support systems, and are governed by the regenerative, creative components of a living process.

In 'being off the world', the relation between three aspects of the process of living—political economy, social structure and culture, and science and knowledge—are asymmetrical and fragmented, because of which the processes of production are discontinuous with the life process. The production process exists 'off' the life-world, taking from it without taking care to not diminish and damage it. Articulation between them, for this reason, is in one direction and not reciprocal, that is, its goal is to conquer nature and subjugate it to the advantage of human beings. This is destructive of the life-support systems.

In 'being off the world', production processes transgress the limits of life processes. Therefore, they move towards capital accumulation and the generation of surplus. The conceptual apparatus of this science cannot satisfactorily address questions of human rights, cultural plurality and identity, and ecological and environmental viability. The processes of material production and distribution are unrelated to the reproduction of social and cultural capital (symbolic goods). For this reason, the life-support system is destroyed.

A caring mode of 'being for the world' builds reciprocity between these three aspects of the process of living: political economy, social structure and culture, and science and knowledge. Here, 'being for the world' is concerned with ensuring the continuity of living processes. From this perspective, life-support systems cannot be defined satisfactorily by either the market or the State, or by both of them put together. The State and the market perpetuate and deepen the contradiction between equity and development. The relations between labour, technology, culture, environment, ecology, human rights, productivity, equity, and work culture are important for the production and reproduction of material and symbolic goods, which ensure the necessary conditions for the recovery of the human capacity for self-regeneration. For this, people need to be engaged not only as numbers or as cultural identities alone, but also as persons with knowledge and skills. Culture includes the experiments undertaken by people to create conditions for self-determination and to correct the asymmetry between equity and development.

The Adivasi Sensibility and Labour Potentiality

Giorgio Agamben (1999) has argued that the structure of potentiality comprises both potentiality and impotentiality (that is, the potentiality not to). Bruno Gulli (2005) similarly says,

> .... potentiality not to, the ability to say no, to withdraw, is freedom itself.... If all concrete labor do not spontaneously make use of their ability to not pass into actuality, it remains the task of a radical ontology of labor to show the viability of such an option, at least at the level of theory; and show that other and better worlds are indeed possible once the logic of exploitation is destroyed, as well as show once again that it is on the shoulders of labor that the global machinery of capital rests.... (p. 6)
>
> ... what remains to be ascertained is whether there is an outside to subsumption and globalization—but this outside does not have to be spatial in character, it is of an ontological and political outside that we are speaking here.... (p. 7)

The suggestion here is that 'once the logic of exploitation (of the process of subsumption and globalization of capital) is destroyed', then the 'not-spatial ontological and political outside' is 'other and better worlds'. Further, that it is labour's ability to 'say no' that makes this possible. The saying 'no' is not a negation; it simultaneously creates time and space for 'other and better worlds'. This seems to be Gulli's idea of a radical ontology of labour. In his discussion on this subject, however, Gulli does not give sufficient attention to the foundation of the processes of subsumption, namely primitive accumulation.

The process of accumulation of capital continues to take from people their means of subsistence. This taking away is the means by which to universalise labour teleology, namely pulling human beings out of the state of nature and annihilating their sense of belonging. This universalises the European culture of modernity by means of three sets of separation: separation of consciousness from conscience, fact from value, and lexical truth from applied praxis.[4] The forcible separation of people from their means of production is not possible without these three separations. The teleology of labour maintains these separations by reproducing them each time that surplus value is reproduced. Thus, teleology directs labour to generate surplus value, accumulate it, and create capital on the one hand, and push all classes of society, that is, the rich, the middle class, and the labouring poor, to internalise these separations on the other.

The ability of labour to 'say no' needs to be read in relation to these separations and their universalisation. Labour can say no to them by creating a dialogue between consciousness and conscience, fact and value, and lexical truth with applied praxis. What is the bearing of Adivasi sensibility on the teleology of labour of primitive accumulation? A close listening makes it clear that the Adivasi sensibility resists and says no to these separations.

Ranajit Guha's study of accounts of insurgencies reported by the British over a period of 117 years, from 1783–1900, provides an idea of the 'elementary aspects' of Adivasi sensibility (Guha 1983). Some of these aspects, selected from the point of view of our discussion, are: discrimination and negation, inversion and ambiguity, the communal process of mobilisation, and the sparing use of violence and territoriality. Guha's interpretation of these accounts is textual, decontextualised, as it were. Guha says,

> .... negations are worked out in terms of two sets of principles—first, which we shall call discrimination, was realized in its most explicit form in the violence selectively directed ... at particular targets ... demonstrated how clearly the peasant distinguished between friend and foe ... in the immediate context and its extension to people and things.... (ibid., 20–27);

> inversion, that is 'to destroy or appropriate for themselves the signs (this included speech, everyday practices, rituals and customs) of the authority of those who dominate them' (ibid., 28);
>
> communal process of mobilization … confer, plan, assemble, attack (ibid., 115–116) … and sparing in their use of this (murder) kind of violence (ibid., 164);
>
> … and territoriality—sense of belonging to a common lineage as well as to a common habitat. (ibid., 279)

With regard to the principle of discrimination, Guha states: 'it is a negative class consciousness in that the definition of class which was involved was that of their enemies rather than of themselves; in other words, the nobility' (Guha 1983, 20). On inversion, he is of the opinion that there is an

> imprint of a consciousness trying to identify some of the basic elements of economic exploitation and political infrastructure.… it is still rather disjointed perception … falls short of conceptualizing the structure of authority which made such conditions possible … one could say after Gramsci the only form in which state is perceived is officialdom.… (ibid., 28)

With regard to the sparing use of murder as a kind of violence, Guha says:

> the answer must be sought in two aspects of rebel consciousness—namely, its inertia and negativity. It was not a liberated consciousness. On the contrary, … it was still trapped in the old culture. That culture imbued the peasant with a sense of reverence for the body of anyone ranked as his superior. For the form of the human body is a symbol, as Hegel said, and its symbolism in the highly semioticized world of traditional India was very potent. (ibid., 164)

Finally, about territoriality, Guha states:

> What is this consciousness which is so bitterly denounced by revolutionaries as a limiting factor of peasant insurgency? It is made up, in its Indian form, of a sense of lineage as well as to a common habitat—an intersection of two primordial referents, which, for

> the purpose of the present discussion, we shall call territoriality. (ibid., 279)

To frame these accounts of insurgency, Guha has creatively interwoven ideas evolved from the Revolutionary Left (D. D. Kosambi, Friedrich Engels, Antonio Gramsci, Henri Lefebvre, Mao, etc.) and social anthropology. The balance is tilted towards the former. What is noticeable is the absence of the works of Rosa Luxemberg, who discussed at length the aspects of primitive accumulation on the one hand and anthropological fieldwork on the other. This is a significant absence. Two very important elements also seem to be missing from his framework. The *first* is the backdrop—the description of the historical landscape created by primitive accumulation, people, and the events to which these insurgents are responding—and *second*, the insurgent's social structure, labour, and existence.

The insurgent Adivasi sensibility as it emerges from Guha's frame has the following elementary aspects. It possesses a negative class consciousness, in that the definition of class relates to the Adivasis' enemies rather than to themselves; it is based on a 'rather disjointed perception', and falls short of conceptualising the structure of authority; it is imbued with inertia and negativity; it is not a liberated consciousness; it possesses a sense of reverence for the body of anyone ranked as their superior; and its sense of territoriality is bitterly denounced by revolutionaries.

A question arises here: Is the revolutionary sensibility party to the ploy of primitive accumulation of pulling people out of the state of nature? The works of social anthropologists, some of which Guha has drawn upon, have shown that there is no such thing as the 'state of nature'. Guha seems to believe that the 'state of nature' can be overcome: that a revolutionary consciousness rooted in the necessity of conceptualising the structure of authority will break the inertia and negativity, and create the ground for a liberated consciousness that would transcend a territoriality limited by the sense of belonging to a lineage and a habitat.

Are these attributes not of the sensibility of primitive accumulation and its underlying teleology of labour? Primitive accumulation also expresses a negative class consciousness that is focused more on its enemies than on itself. It separates consciousness from conscience; it is based on a rather disjointed perception of authority, where there is a separation of fact from value, and for this reason it falls short of conceptualsing its structure. It is unable to reflect on its self, and for this reason it shows a high level of inertia and concomitant negativity. Another instance of its inability to conceptualise is its failure to see that the sense of reverence for the dead bodies of those ranked as superior is not possible without a sense of reverence for everyone's bodies. The bitter denunciation by revolutionaries of insurgents' sense of belonging and territoriality is a reflection of it not being a liberated consciousness; this denunciation emerges from the separation of lexical truth from applied praxis. That is to say, the theory of revolutionary consciousness is not linked with the practices (that are embedded in the social structure, work, and existence) of the insurgents.

It is worthwhile to consider a different way of reading insurgents' sensibility. The ability to differentiate between enemy and friend demonstrates that the consciousness and conscience are linked, and in dialogue. A consciousness of their enemies is not possible without a clear understanding of themselves. The clarity of perception regarding the relation between fact and value that underlies the structure of authority informs 'inversion'; without such clarity, inversion would not be possible. The sparing use of murder as a kind of violence does not hint at inertia and negativity; rather, it demonstrates a sense of restraint. The territoriality embedded in the sense of belonging is different from the sense of territoriality of primitive accumulation, which murders recklessly and indiscriminately and destroys any sense of belonging. Further, the bitter denouncement of the insurgent sense of territoriality begs the question: What is the nature of the revolutionary consciousness that is uprooted, and that has no sense of belonging?

It is important to draw attention to the Adivasi insurgent's relationship with the revolutionaries. In post-independent India, revolutionary political forces of diverse persuasions have endeavoured to provide leadership to the Adivasi people. Simultaneously, there has been a very strong desire amongst Adivasis to say 'no' to any form of assimilation, accompanied by an openness to show solidarity with other peoples. R. D. Munda and S. Bosu Mullick (2003) point out that the people have

> ... successfully nullified the predictions of both the bourgeois and classical Marxist schools of thought that the aboriginal's last act will be squalid, instead of being tragic. What will be seen with most regret will be, not his disappearance, but his enslavement and degradation and that 'such national groups (are) non-historic' ... who were 'lacking national vitality and condemned to disappear or prone to be denationalised....' (Munda and Mullick 2003, 269)
>
> ... years of struggle against different forms of colonial forces the peoples have experienced all the three options—negation-isolation-tragedy; surrender-assimilation-squalid; and equilibrium of rejection-accommodation-symbiosis-integration.... (ibid., 270)
>
> The people have always remained open to 'direct change' but what they have opposed is assimilation.... Their age-old wisdom, manifested in their daily practices even today, upholds the human approach of integration with other peoples within the same political and social framework.... In the early days, every lineage group separately fought against the alien forces. Later on different combinations of joint efforts emerged and very soon there evolved a pan-indigenous unity. And finally, a broad-based unity of the indigenous peoples, peasantry, and artisan communities was reached at. (ibid., 270–271)

Adivasis resisted efforts at assimilation by the left revolutionaries as much as those of right-wing and liberal politics, but remained open to issue-based alliances.

What holds them back is their restraint concerning violence in politics, their sense of belonging to lineage and habitat, and their understanding of the political structures of the State that they were struggling against. The left is no different from the right or the liberal political forces with regard to their policy on minerals, forests, and other natural resources, and on the question of militarisation and industrial development.

This mode of Adivasi insurgency is not about a 'negation' of revolutionary politics, but is about 'saying no' to absolute inclusion within parliamentary political processes, saying no to armed political struggles, and to development processes that undermine the gifts of nature. They are not opposed to modernisation, but to their subordination to the rationale of the dominant systems in the world. The Adivasi sensibility that resists assimilation has been described as a 'sense of autonomy' and 'self-rule'. The insurgency that emerges from this sensibility seeks broad-based alliances with the working class of people who respect nature's gifts, desires friendships across inequalities, and is grounded in a sense of belonging to lineage and habitat. The formation of the state of Jharkhand in 2000 is an expression of this sensibility. Other instances are to be found in experiments in 'autonomy and self-rule', two of which are briefly described here.

One instance, described by Ritambhara Hebbar (2011), is of how the Ho people of Mirra village in West Singhbhum district in Jharkhand took on the responsibility of looking after the forest.

> ... Some of the young villagers ... were upset by the idea of hiring outsiders for a job that could be performed by villagers. In retaliation, they cut down trees, which were marked out for the purpose of silkworm rearing. So, the concern over forest involved introspection on such acts of violence against the forest, wherein villagers were involved in aggravating the problem of degradation by cutting forest. They found themselves behaving like the forest department by disrespecting the forest and setting an aggressive relation with it.... They expressed distress over the rate of degradation and felt that not only will the villagers of Mirra suffer if this continues, but so will the villagers around it....
>
> ... The formation of VRDs (Van Raksha Dals/Forest Protection Groups), then involved a reflection on two important aspects regarding the forest: (a) control, i.e., who should be in charge of the forest and (b) what should be the methods and techniques that should be employed to restore the forest ... whether the forest should be rejuvenated along the principles set around tradition by respecting the boundaries of spirits.... or should they adopt modern principles of forest rejuvenation whereby the rate of reproduction of forest is sought to be altered by introducing fast growing trees, hybrid seeds, etc? (ibid., 202–204)

Hebbar points out that a significant area of contention between the three Van Raksha Dals was whether or not to establish a relation with the Tata Steel Rural Development Society (TSRDS); they feared that taking the help of the TSRDS could involve a compromise with their independence. The co-existence of these Dals kept the tension in the village alive. Each point of view was provided a space within the dynamics of day-to-day life.

> Differences, in this sense, are a field for contest and transgression. Thus, it is through transgression that villagers experiment with self-rule to constitute themselves as 'subjects' and at the same time, to restore the forest.... (Hebbar 2011, 206).
>
> The 'self' and the 'other' are constituted within the village space not only at the level of personal differences and village politics, but also at the level of their understanding and management of the forest. (ibid., 208)

Another instance reported by Martina Claus and Sebastian Hartig (2018) concerns the struggle against the Koel Karo hydroelectric project. A hydel project was proposed on the rivers Koel and Karo, about 80 km southwest of the capital Ranchi in the state of Jharkhand. The project area was at an average altitude of 480 m and included the districts of Singhbum, Gumla, and Ranchi, which are mainly inhabited by the Adivasi Mundas and Oraons. This project was to generate 710 megawatts of electricity via different constructions distributed throughout the aforementioned districts. The survey work, carried out by the Bihar State Electricity Board, had already commenced in the years 1956–1957. According to the Koel Karo Jan Sangathan (KKJS), 256 villages with a total population of 150,000, primarily Adivasi, would have been affected by the project.

Further, they point out that the people of the Koel Karo area had been living in constant threat and insecurity since the beginning of the project in the 1950s. This pressure resulted in a lack of investment in land, because people feared losing their property to the dam. The people concentrated their energy towards compelling the government to abandon the dam project. The period of resistance was very difficult. Younger people took on the time-consuming work in the resistance movement while also supporting their families financially.

The announcement of the closure of the project motivated the people to become autonomous, form co-operatives for collective decision-making, and create the opportunity to design and implement their own plans for development in the area, in the domains of education, health, agriculture, sustainable forestry, and fishery. They had plans for irrigation systems, water reservoirs, and the construction of small hydroelectric projects that would not displace the population. In addition, the area has seen the construction of a Munda school and vocational training institutes, as well as the cultivation of fruit-bearing trees and other economically productive plants. Further, there was a plan to focus special attention on and provide developmental assistance to support the victims' families. All this contributed to strengthening solidarity among the village community, and also inspired other villages to join the development strategies of the KKJS.

Summing up

The Adivasi sensibility in India has emerged from the hard work of insurgency over 200 years. It gives expression to the creative potential of 'insurgent energy'. It is grounded in the active principle of labour, namely its ability to say no, to withdraw, to retreat and reflect on the conditions of its possibility. The indigenous perspective and the Adivasi sensibility may have emerged in different historical contexts, but they share a common concern, that is, to explore the human labour potential outside the framework and processes of the primitive accumulation of capital.

Endnotes

1. In 1867, Marx (*Capital*, Vol. 1) pointed out that

> The so-called primitive accumulation, therefore, is nothing else than the historical process of divorcing the producer from the means of production.... In the history of primitive accumulation, all revolutions are epoch-making that act as levers for the capital class in course of formation; but, above all, those moments when great masses of men are suddenly and forcibly torn from their means of subsistence, and hurled as free and unattached

proletarians on the labour-market. The expropriation of the agricultural producer, of the peasant, from the soil, is the basis of the whole process.

2. 'Among American Indian people, centuries of genocidal child removal policies remain fresh in our minds. We remember our children were taken away from us by white society to facilitate assimilation and because we are viewed as essentially inferior, lazy, alcoholic, and inherently unable to care for our children' (Poupart 2003, 94). The Germans viewed the 'Nama to be lazy good-for-nothing. Hence, they devised a deportation scheme and aimed at the eventual extinction of the Nama' (Berat 1993, 23. fn 110). '.... It was a cornerstone of the Nazi demonization of Jews that they were essentially a parasitic class, incapable of "honest" work and thus driven to usury, lazy cosmopolitanism, and criminality'. See 'The Jewish Holocaust', p. 265. Available at http://www.genocidetext.net/gaci_holocaust.pdf (accessed May 2023).

3. For a discussion on this subject, see Popke (2003).

4. These separations are discussed in Uberoi (2002).

Five

Caretakers and Conquerors*

While in the USA, New Zealand, and South America the distinction between the indigenous people and the alien outsiders has been easy to make, in India it has not been so easy. There have been several waves of culturally diverse people coming from different parts of the world, intermingling over several generations and belonging equally to the place. For this reason, the parameter of the historically and chronologically 'first' or culturally 'original' does not hold for India.

However, there are similarities in the way colonisers defined indigenous people in other parts of the world and the forest dwellers in India. The society and culture of these people were described by colonial anthropology as 'primitive'—small-scale kinship communities living in isolation, earning their livelihood by means of shifting cultivation, food gathering, and hunting. The intention behind such characterisation was mainstreaming the people and integrating them into the world of industrial development.

This mainstreaming, however, was oppressive. There were substantial differences in the magnitude of oppression—the indigenous people in Africa and the continents of North and South America suffered genocide, while the Maoris in New Zealand suffered linguistic annihilation. In India, the forest people (whom the British called 'tribal') have a long history of protest. The colonial policy

*An earlier version of this chapter was published as 'Nature, Deforestation and Conservation: An Indigenous Discourse', in *Contemporary Perspectives: History and Sociology of South Asia* 2 (2), July-December 2008. New Delhi: Sage Publications.

adopted by Independent India evolved to civilising by means of legal marginalisation and subsequent integration.

The encounter and relation between the forest dwellers and the mainstream in India have three aspects. The first emerged from the forest people's own initial response to the alien colonial intrusion. Indigenous opposition to the mainstream came much before the non-indigenous people initiated the constitutional struggle for independence under the leadership of the Indian National Congress (INC), which was formed in 1885 on the initiative of the British. The second aspect emerged gradually with the combination of development programmes—Sanskritisation with the Hindus and Westernisation with Christian missionaries mainstreamed the forest dwellers and gave them a tribal identity. As a result tribals are not forest dwellers.[1] The third aspect emerged when the Church in the Northeast adopted tribal customary practices. That is, instead of either total acceptance or rejection, people's response is selective and situational to development interventions.[2] These responses all say, what once used to be traditional is now becoming modern (Hirtz 2003).

The forest dwelling tribal people in India and the indigenous people in different continents are witnessing that mainstream efforts continue to destroy their sense of belonging to a place by taking away their land, forests, and waterways for purposes of militarisation; through the formation of nuclear States; the building of large dams; and the construction of reserves of nature.

As international development decisions affect tribal people in India, their participation on international platforms has also increased. How do we see the convergence of the tribal-indigenous response?[3] What is this indigenousness that brings the indigenous and the tribal people together? This chapter highlights the difference between caretakers' reflexivity and conquerors' instrumentalism.

Indigenousness

Benedict Kingsbury (1998) argues that even though there are differences regarding the meaning and applicability of the term 'indigenous', it is worth the effort to continue to work with it:

> ... it is a concept of great normative power for many relatively powerless groups that have suffered grievous abuses, and it bears the imprimatur of representatives of many such groups.... As a concept designating a locus of groups and issues, albeit with some imprecision and uncertainties, it has proved remarkably serviceable, and there is no contending replacement.... (Kingsbury 1998, 415)

This, according to him, requires a recognition of the fact that 'perfect positivist coherence is unachievable'. This is because the legal terminology requires a precise definition and

> Once established, such definitions theoretically ground the interpretive process of determining the scope of application.... Any strict definition ... will tend to reduce the fluidity and dynamism of social life.... (ibid., 414)

A second 'constructivist' approach, Kingsbury argues, takes

> the international concept of 'indigenous peoples' not as one sharply defined by universally applicable criteria, but as embodying a continuous process in which claims and practices in numerous specific cases are abstracted in the wider institutions of society, then made specific again at the moment of application in the political, legal and social processes of particular cases and societies. (ibid., 415)

Perhaps the normative power of the concept is embedded in the deeper meaning of the terms 'origin' and 'first',[4] and also in the historical experience of oppression. The term 'indigenous' draws attention to the relation of people to a place and to a sense of belonging. The use of the term 'primitive' indicates an outsider's intrusion into and forcible occupation of land and territory. The term 'indigenous' thus suggests decolonisation, and subsequent uses of the term have lent it greater depth. The term 'indigenous' was used for the first time in 1920 by the ILO to bring justice to 'native workers'; this is in contrast to the term 'primitive', which is used to legitimise unjust practices.

The ILO was set up in 1919 and one of its first studies was concerned with indigenous workers. In 1926, the Governing Body created a Committee of Experts on native workers, which discussed penal sanctions for any breach of contract by the employed indigenous workers (Simpson 1939, 719). The ILO Convention 107 (1957) was inclusive of indigenous and tribal populations. Even though the major initiative for the Convention came from the Americas, it attracted the interest of several African and Asian States.[5] In 1971, the UN Commission on Human Rights appointed Jose R. Martinez Cobo as Special Rapporteur to conduct its first ever study of indigenous people. The study identified a rootedness in land as the primary marker of indigenous identity (Clech Lam 2004, 29).

> Cobo's description captured the fundamental and unchanging message that indigenous delegates from around the world carried, beginning in the 1960s, to international fora where they seek international legal and institutional protection, impelled by the depredations of global capitalism in the territories as well as by the attendant impotence if not connivance of their enclosing states. The message indigenous people deliver is a simple one: their ability to survive as distinct peoples is inextricably tied to their right to occupy their traditional territories and control their resources ... indigenous ... claiming territoriality an attribute normally associated with sovereign statehood or independence to which, paradoxically, only a few aspire. (ibid., 130)

With the emergence of the human rights movement during the 1970s, the culture of the workplace was defined not only by technology, but also by labour. Thus, labour could not be understood without taking into account people's social and cultural practices. During the 1980s, indigenous peoples all over the world were engaged in struggles against invasions and genocide, militarisation, the formation of nuclear States, mining, large dams, reckless commercial forestry, pollution, missionaries, modern education, racism, the exploitation of labour, forcible sterilisation of women, unjust imprisonment, tourism, and the forced sale of land (Moody 1988). In 1981, the UNESCO Declaration in San Jose condemned ethnocide, and opened the way for ethno-development in keeping with the rights of indigenous peoples. [6] The San Jose text states:

The key propositions in this declaration are:

> ... ethnocide, that is, cultural genocide, is a violation of international law equivalent to genocide, which was condemned by the United Nations Convention on the Prevention and Punishment of the Crime of Genocide of 1948. (Proposition 1)
>
> ... ethno-development is an inalienable right of Indian groups. (Proposition 2).
>
> ... By ethno-development we mean the extension and consolidation of the elements of its own culture, through strengthening the independent decision-making capacity of a culturally distinct society to direct its own development and exercise self-determination, at whatever level, which implies an equitable and independent share of power. This means that the ethnic group is a political and administrative unit, with authority over its own territory and decision-making powers within the confines of its development project, in a process of increasing autonomy and self-management. (Proposition 3)
>
> ... Since the European invasion, the Indian peoples of America have seen their history denied or distorted, despite their great contributions to the progress of mankind, which has led to the negation of their very existence. We reject this unacceptable misrepresentation. (Proposition 4)
>
> .... The Indian peoples have a natural and inalienable right to the territories they possess as well as the right to recover the land taken away from them. This implies the right to the natural and cultural heritage that this territory contains. (Proposition 7)
>
> .... Respect for the forms of autonomy required by the Indian peoples is an essential condition for guaranteeing and implementing these. (Proposition 9)
>
> .... Furthermore, the Indian people's own forms of internal organization are part of their cultural and legal heritage which has contributed to their cohesion and to maintaining their socio-cultural traditions. (Proposition 10) (UNESCO 1981).

Even though the San Jose declaration was initiated by the Latin American indigenous people and also referred to their history and understanding of cultural ethnocide, it drew attention to the genocide/ethnocide of other minority communities in other parts of the world as well. The meaning of 'indigenous', according to the declaration, is embedded in the relation of belonging (as distinct from invasion and conquest), and the sense of being in the world and the territory. In 1989, spurred by the growing criticisms of integration and assimilation, a revised version of Convention 107 was formulated, as Convention 169. This Convention was adopted in 1989 and was enforced in 1991.[7]

This Convention stipulated that

> self-identification as indigenous or tribal shall be regarded as fundamental criterion for determining the groups to which the provisions of this Convention apply and the peoples concerned shall have the right to decide their own priorities for the process of development as it affects their lives, beliefs, institutions and spiritual well-being and the lands they occupy or otherwise use, and to exercise control, to the extent possible, over their own economic, social and cultural development. In addition, they shall participate in the formulation, implementation and evaluation of plans and programs for national and regional development which may affect them directly.[8]

During the 1980s and 1990s, the agenda for destructive development, which had monopolised natural resources, undermined ecology and denied access to the people. Displacement and rehabilitation gradually became a part of the development agenda. By the beginning of the twenty-first century, it was clear that this agenda was to continue. These and other related developments reinforce the indigenous message across the world—that territoriality is not just about land and social formations, nor is it just about constructions of identity. These are the grounds for a just being in the world with a sense of belonging.

Over time, cultural minorities in Europe[9] and South Asia (Clarke 2001) came to share a common cause—to identify the genocide element in development and oppose it.

This made the term 'indigenous' inclusive (and not confined to a purely chronological determination of who the first settlers were)[10] of tribal people from all countries in Asia and Africa, alongside those in North and South America and Australia. Gradually, there was awareness that the

> 'just struggle of indigenous people is closely tied to the struggle of peasants for land and of workers for better living conditions' throughout the developing world. From this it emerged gradually that 'the policies and programmes which allowed people to determine their place in society and, the place of their culture and tradition in that society' are preferable to assimilation. (Barsh 1986, 377–378)

Since the historical experience of genocide/ethnocide and ecocide cannot be fully translated into the 'claims and practices' referred to by Kingsbury, indigenousness is pitted against processes of systemic destruction (Kingsbury 1998). In this context of mass destruction, it becomes important to know what it is that is one's own and what it means to stand up for it. It is inclusive of everyone who has contributed time to making a place worthy of belonging to, and of knowing the living interconnections with other beings. Ancestors are not necessarily people with whom a person or a group can demonstrate a genealogical bloodline. They constitute generational labour time as well as the labour time of natural landscapes in the long duration. Generational labour is embedded in care and is an important constituent of indigenousness.

Caretakers and Indigenousness

This section is based on conversations with Koitors in Abujhmarh, North Bastar, Chattisgarh and Hill Kharias in Similipal Biosphere Reserve, Koraput, Odisha. These people have not sought to become a part of the mainstream. They stay away, and this counts as radical assertion. The villages I visited in these regions are at a considerable distance from the cities and towns. Here social life, enveloped by dense forest, breathes along with plants and animals. People see their world along with them through a variety of niches, and the canopy brings light from the sun, moon, and stars.

Distance continues to inhibit the frequency of visits and large flows of people. Unlike in the past, village people go to towns and townspeople, largely traders, government officials, political party representatives, NGOs, social movement activists, religious proselytisers, and students and researchers, come in occasionally.

Koitors observe several changes over the past two generations—depletion of the area available for shifting cultivation because of government encroachment on forests; decrease in the time available for forest regeneration; restrictions placed on access to the forest by government legislation, and recently by armed confrontations between the State and Maoists. Increasingly, erratic rainfall, lowering of the groundwater level, government propaganda in favour of a settled rice agriculture for which there was insufficient land, and the demarcation of territory for mega projects, which has also led to the depletion of forest land for livelihood.

They also described instances of injustices suffered. Development officers have acquired the habits of careless work, behaving badly with women, and taking away their poultry forcefully. Koitors were distressed with the schools, where their children were compelled to not speak in their mother tongue, which results in their returning home to become a burden, because they refused to contribute to any work at home. They ask their families for money and look down upon their elders' way of life in the forest. In recent times, there are reports of increasing fear because of an escalation in armed confrontation, which undermines their cultural activities and customary practices.

On one occasion several years ago, in order to assert their point of view, when the district magistrate of Bastar visited a village, the Koitors placed before him on one side 'several' leaf cups, each with one variety of rice, and on the other side, 'one' leaf cup with several varieties of seeds. They explained that one leaf cup with several varieties of seeds represents one shifting cultivation field on a hillside, where a variety of crops could be harvested. It was most suited to the soil and topography of the forested hills, and was a part of their cultural traditions and institutional structures. In contrast, the several leaf cups represented rice cultivation fields. Each leaf cup stood for one flat rice field where only one rice variety could be harvested. It thus required a large quantity of flat land. They further pointed out that in their experience, there was insufficient flat land and for this reason, the rice economy of wage labour was both unstable and unsustainable. The Koitors' preference for shifting cultivation did not, however, register with the magistrate.

The worldview of shifting cultivation that was presented before the district magistrate has been shaped along the contours of work done by mother earth. The Koitors see this as the original labor which makes life itself possible. The epic of their origin, which is sung over several days, begins with a description of a sad Talurmuttee—Mother Earth—sitting on a hilltop looking at the forest submerged under floodwater. The epic goes on to describe the work she does to recover the forest and transform it into a living space—which is both a home and a place of work. This is a description of the original labour, that is, the work of nature.[11] Talurmuttee taught her companion Kanga, the forest ancestor of the Koitors, the arts and crafts of living in a forest. Amongst other things, Kanga learnt shifting cultivation, making a home, and collecting food and medicinal plants.

The oral tradition records forty-eight years of the shifting cultivation cycle. A forest cleared once for cultivation was left fallow for forty-eight years. The forest that was cleared had a high canopy and low undergrowth. After the shifting cultivation harvest, the forest cycles begin afresh—from thick vegetation on the ground with no canopy to sparse vegetation on the ground and a high canopy. This is fallow time, for self-regeneration and self-activity of nature.

One harvest lasted roughly for at least two lunar years. A fresh clearance was made every third lunar year. In other words, a new cultivation cycle would begin every third lunar year. In this manner, cultivation rotates over twenty-four fields, and then return along the same pathway. All clearings cultivated in succession during these years had the same fallow regeneration time.

At the centre of this system and process was a sacred forest, the abode of mother earth. This is where her shrine was located. Before beginning to 'clear' forest land for cultivation and before eating the fresh harvest, all the men in the village would make offerings to mother earth; this was a way of expressing gratitude for her work. In this sacred forest, not even a leaf could be plucked. Only that which falls on the ground (dry leaves, wood, ripe fruits, etc.) could be gathered. A comparison between the biodiversity in the sacred forest and that in the clearings showed the changes in the vegetation in the latter, brought about on account of cultivation. This contrast was meaningful at different levels of their social life.

The reproduction time-cycles of forest materials—mud, bamboo, trees, plants, animals, and insects—set the time for human activity. It shaped notions of generational depth, the lifecycles of settlements, everyday time, cultivation time, and time for the collection of food and medicine.

The notion of 'mother earth' as it is referred to in the oral tradition describes 'self-regeneration', or the self-activity of nature, as an aspect of the feminine principle. This underlies the relations of the people to the forest as a whole, and to each of the 'clearances'. In keeping with this principle, the forest is a three-dimensional space. The feminine aspect gives the forest a canopy, height, a variety of life forms, volume, and depth. It cannot be owned because it is not a product of human labour. This is the obverse of the labour theory of value. It is for this reason that the sacred forest, referred to earlier, belongs to no human being, as it is the creation of the 'work of nature'—hence the prohibition to not pluck even a stray leaf. Only that which is invested with human labour can be owned by human beings, and thus a clearing in the forest and the harvest are both the work of humans.

However, fallow regeneration or the self-activity of nature dissolves this work of human beings. For this reason, as the clearing gradually returns to the forest, it comes under the care of the community (which comprises all the families that are part of the settlement).[12] An important aspect of care is non-interference with the time meant for recuperation and regeneration.

I learnt a different perception of the forest from the food gatherers, the Hill Kharias, the indigenous people in the Similipal Biosphere Reserve. In their worldview, the tiger is not at the apex of the forest ecosystem. According to the Kharias, who are now few in number and were once famous for honey collection, the forest is designed for the subtle work of making honey. There is no king of the forest. The forest is a magical manifestation of the feminine principle. It is the abode of mother earth. There is a queen of the forest, the Queen Bee. She is at the apex of the forest ecosystem.

There was a time not long ago—seventy years, approximately—when honey was collected in abundance. There were several full honey reservoirs. According to the descriptions I was given, these were dispersed across the forest landscape and were found at all levels, from the undergrowth to the canopy (and were not concentrated in any one region). I saw a large one near *athradeoli* (or Athara Deula), a sacred grove in the core area of Similipal Biosphere Reserve. There is another one visible from the forest road mid-way in the buffer zone. The system of collecting honey in the past, as narrated to me by a *Dehori* (the priest of the sacred grove and a medicine man) is as follows.

The rights of collecting honey from different reservoirs were distributed over different Kharia lineages. This right extended to the collection of other forest produce, but no further than the region covered by the bees. The queen of all varieties of bees was the Bagho Machi or the tiger bee (perhaps the cliff bee in English). This Kharia name draws attention to their capability to kill a tiger. Their hives, created on the steep waterfall hillside, are wet and slippery and are accessible to no one other than a trustworthy husband-and-wife team of honey collectors. Their interdependence in everyday life laid the strong foundations for a trust that was necessary in the difficult and risky task of climbing down to the hive. The man would be suspended down the slippery cliff by a rope held by his wife. Any breach of trust meant death. The collection process was punctuated with rituals and ceremonies to propitiate the Queen Bee, without which honey collection was impossible. Any change in the ecology of the forest is reflected in honey production. The quality of honey at each level tells the story of the forest at that particular level. A good honey collector will glean the health of the forest from the quantity, texture, smell, and colour of the honey.

I was told by the Kharias that the tiger walks and circumscribes the forest to prevent outsiders from disturbing the making of honey. Like other forest dwellers, Kharias know that the tiger's transgression into human settlements points to a disturbance in the relation between the people and mother earth. This prompts an audit of the procedures of harvesting and gathering of food. They look for violation(s) of rules. The most important rules are: *first*, no fruit will be plucked or crop harvested before it is ripe. *Second*, before beginning the cultivation cycle, the village collective has to propitiate mother earth. *Third*, when the harvesting is complete, a collective thanksgiving to mother earth ends the cultivation cycle, and no one will eat the harvested food-crop until it has been offered to mother earth.

This narrative draws attention to the Kharias' view that the forest is a network regulated by honeybees. Their distribution at all levels, from the ground to the canopy, unifies the forest. Another aspect of care is interdependence.

The possibility of shifting cultivation and of honey collection is embedded in the ability to listen to and read the forest. This is the basis of their ability to identify plants in any season, and from any part (and not just the flower). For instance,

> residents of one forest village in Thailand eat 295 different local plants and use another 119 for medicine. The World Health Organization estimates that 3,000 plant species are used for birth control by tribal people around the world. (World Resources 1992–1993, 135)
>
> It is estimated that 2,65,000 flowering species grace the earth. Of these, less than half of 1 percent have been studied exhaustively for their chemical composition and medicinal value. In a world with limited financial resources, it is impossible to screen each of the remaining species for biological activity. Some kind of collection strategy is needed. (Cox and Balick 1994)

Without the cognitive and laboratory equipment of modern science, how do forest people know the properties of plants? Indeed, there is a great difference in the way forest people access nature through their daily activities. Their institutions give them the space and time to feel and learn from the touch of nature. Shifting cultivation, honey collection, and the recognition of plants have two interconnected components, namely the work of humans and the work of nature. They are arranged to complement and supplement each other. Together, they constitute the indigenous labour that makes a forest living space a dwelling—a habitation, a place to live in, and also a space to dwell on. Koitors and Kharias dwell in and dwell on the universe of the forest. On this rests the possibility of living in (dwelling in) the forest as well as the capability to see clearings (dwelling on); in this way, the forest evokes an imagination, a way of thinking and contemplation that clears the ground for living in it.

The generational depth (of several generations) of this labour, discernible in the social and cultural practices of the people, has three aspects: *first*, the creative work of recognising, identifying, classifying, selecting, and processing observations; *second*, craftsmanship, to build homes and earn a livelihood; and *third*, the construction of institutions, social spaces, sacred geographies, customs, legends, rituals, and traditions of learning and transmission. These aspects are shaped by the forest time cycles, cultivation practices, and the materials used for daily living.

In the view of the Koitors and the Hill Kharias, the quality and quantity of forest regeneration time shapes social time and space. For instance, on account of forest regeneration, an abandoned settlement returns to the forest after a couple of years, in the same way as a forest returns on a fallow clearing. This is the same as saying that the lifecycle of plants and animals shapes the contours of human activity; the most elementary and yet the most important of them all is the activity of observation, that is, the ability to see and record.

To sum up, care is integral to the mutually regenerative relation between forest dwellers and mother earth. Nature needs human beings as much as human beings need nature. It is for this reason that human beings are a part of nature and nature is a part of human beings. This is a core aspect of indigenousness.

Conquerors

In the course of my work with the Koitors, there were several occasions on which I was asked to explain from my perspective the changes that people had observed. I found the story of Gilgamesh (Sandars 1972 [1960]) appropriate for this. This is an epic concerning the origins of deforestation, a contrast to the epic of Talurmuttee. Some significant parts of the Gilgamesh epic (Savyasaachi 2005, 5) are discussed here.

Gilgamesh said to his servant (Enkidu):

> '... we will go to the forest and destroy the evil; for in the forest lives Humbaba whose name is "Hugeness", a ferocious giant.
>
> It is not an equal struggle when one fights with Humbaba; he is a great warrior, a battering ram.... Follow me, for I know the place where Humbaba lives and the paths he walks....' said Enkidu....
>
> Humbaba said, 'Enkidu, what you have spoken is evil; you a hireling, dependent for your bread! In envy and for fear of a rival you have spoken evil words'.
>
> Enkidu said, 'Do not listen, Gilgamesh: this Humbaba must di....'
>
> Gilgamesh listened to the word of his companion, and he struck Humbaba with a thrust of the sword to the neck, and Enkidu his comrade struck the second blow. At the third blow Humbaba fell. Then there followed confusion for this was the guardian of the forest whom they had felled to the ground....
>
> So they pressed into the forest.... They uncovered the sacred dwelling of the Anunnaki and while Gilgamesh felled the first trees of the forest Enkidu cleared their roots as far as the banks of Euphrates. They set Humbaba before the gods, before Enlil.... Enlil raged at them 'Why did you do this thing? From henceforth may the fire be on your faces, may it eat the bread you eat, may it drink where you drink.'

In contrast to Talurmuttee, Gilgamesh performs the original labour of deforestation, which is a manifestation of his restlessness, his incapacity to contain his energy, and his incapability to make a fair judgment. The clearing of the forest marked the passage from the darkness of evil to the darkness of the curse pronounced by Enlil. It provoked the rage of Enlil, the Sumerian God of earth, wind, and the universal air, ultimately of the spirit, and the executive of Anu. In Sumerian cosmogony, Enlil was born of the union of An, heaven, and Ki, earth. He separated them and carried off the earth as his portion.

The epic of the origins of deforestation can be read as follows: In the beginning, Gilgamesh placed man outside the realm of nature. This is at the core of deforestation. This epic enables a literary reading of enlightenment as a deforestation project. In my reading, this epic describes the origin of modern man. Later, European

Enlightenment constructed instruments to carry forward the work started by Gilgamesh. It developed a notion of reason and with its instrumentality, an industrial technology that gave a structure, system, and process to 'Gilgameshian' restlessness and universalised it. Philosophies were constructed to legitimise industrial production based on the extraction of natural resources and the extrication of 'man' from the 'clutches' of nature. The underlying intentionality to free humans (an absolute release from natural determinations) undermined the feminine principle. In the making of this foundational construct, nature was 'taken for granted', and not given the space to 'present itself as such'. That is to say, the ideas and categories used to develop this construct (of nature and freedom) derived from the negation of nature.

In sixteenth and seventeenth-century Europe, as the mind, spirit, and social institutions were 'freed' from religious rituals, ceremonies, and related practices, nature appeared in its astronomical scale, its unfathomable depths, and its rich variety. This challenged the human spirit and imagination, which had been similarly freed from religious dogmatism. Faced with this challenge, the human imagination initiated the process of self-understanding and self-knowing. Initially, the sense of freedom was intelligible to the imagination in terms of an adventure into the vastness of nature, and also in terms of the ability to return home, rest, recollect, and share the experience and learning with fellow beings.

How far could the imagination go into space and time on the surface as well as into the cosmos? At what depth could it hold on and see? What did it bring back? How was the experience processed? In what form was it to be shared?

In the beginning was the 'word' of reason. It anchored and gave expression to these concerns of the imagination that had been freed from the control of the pulpit. To generate the means (technology) and bear the costs (economic, social, and political) for 'the imagination's new engagement with adventure and freedom', the industrial system and the industrial society evolved. The learnings from explorations were constructed as scientific knowledge—the taxonomical systems of botany and zoology, for instance. The magic of the spheres was now rewritten as the planetary system.

The process to generate these means began with the industrial revolution. It sped up and transformed four basic components of a productive activity: the extraction of raw materials from nature; their processing through the production system to make a product; distribution and consumption of the product; and the cycling of residues (waste materials generated all along the production, distribution, and consumption cycle). In contrast to shifting cultivation, which allows more time for regeneration in relation to the time of production, in industrial production this ratio is reversed—the speed at which natural resources are extracted is several times faster than that of its regeneration. This generated residues that could not be recycled, neither by nature nor by man, for example, deep craters left after mining minerals and monoculture plantations for forest produce, and the damming of river waters. This was one of the primary manifestations of the foundational construct. It continues to be such even today. The 'progressive' increase over time in the differential between the rate of extraction and the rate of self-regeneration is a structural component of industrial production. This is a primary contradiction.

Deforestation is the manifestation of this contradiction. The modern production system undermined its own resource base, which is its ground for existence—it increased the speed of destruction of large areas of forest, of several valuable plants and animal species, of fresh air and water, and the occurrence of natural disasters. All these are manifestations of a primary contradiction—in the effort to create better living conditions, the basic conditions for the survival of life itself are undermined on the one hand, and the science and technology used for constructing this 'better life' has generated problems that are beyond its capability to resolve.

In the 1970s, it was realised that the magnitude of these transformations was alarming and threatened not just the sustainability of industrial production, but life itself. This industrial crisis was labelled an 'environmental crisis', so as to not discuss the inherent contradictions of industrial production on the one hand and to prepare the ground for work on more effective ways of generating raw material resources on the other. This intention was clearly visible in the complete reversal of the perception of indigenous knowledge. The earlier position of the 1960s had been that the knowledge and the way of life of the 'first people' were worthless and unscientific. Now, although both became very important for industrial sustainability, the attitude towards the indigenous way of life remained unchanged.

This awareness came in the wake of the rapid mass production and diversification of consumer goods. With similar rapidity, differences led to multiple conflicts, and conflicts degenerated into violence, war, and terrorism. The production of weapons, justified in the name of security, escalated. This further magnified the scale of destruction, augmented the aggressiveness of industrial interest, pushed many more people to the margins—unemployed, displaced, without access to education—and strengthened the resolve of the industrial regime to destroy any 'other' knowledge system by annihilating the conditions for their production and reproduction.

In this context, conservation was conceptualised for a sustainable industrial political economy (without changing its speed) and to protect species life; that is, 'protect' what remains, 'prevent' further loss, and recover species as well as nature-scapes wherever possible. Our interest here is with initiatives for the conservation of forest biodiversity—project shifting cultivation, project 'reserves of nature', and project ethnobotany. These projects illustrate the political economy of 'conservation'. They continued to take away tribal-indigenous ancestral grounds, their livelihoods, and their ways of life to sustain the speed of industrial production. These conservation strategies have augmented the process of capital accumulation and have abetted the rapid rate of technological innovation for mass production, which is directly related to the rapid rate of extracting a large quantity of raw materials needed from nature.

Each of these projects was designed by the mainstream to take control over a large portion of the world's natural resources and displace the indigenous people forcefully from the resource-rich areas they lived in. The perception of nature, deforestation, and conservation underlying the structure and constitution of these projects derived from processes of industrial production and reproduction.

In this context, the discouraging of the practice of shifting cultivation was designed to minimise, and over time eliminate, the use of the forest by forest dwellers, displace them out of the forest, and build 'reserves of nature'. These reserves are large enclosures of forested areas. Ethnobotany collects plants from these reserves to extract genetic material for commercial use. The practice was labelled as being 'destructive' of forests in relation to population growth. It was pointed out that as cycles of cultivation shorten, the fallow time decreases, resulting in deforestation. However, Koitors point out that the shortening of cycles was due to State encroachment on the forest. I was witness to the shifting of boundaries during cadastral surveys—wooden pegs that are aligned to mark the boundaries were shifted by an angle of approximately 15 degrees to include more of the forest. Another method of encroachment is through the declaration of a 'reserved forest'.

At this point in our discussion, we need to recall the presentation made by the Koitors to the district magistrate (described earlier)—they were making a request to view shifting cultivation in its own terms, that is, with reference to the minimal conditions required for its sustainability. Any system of production would be rendered sick if its minimal conditions are not met. The district magistrate could not comprehend this point. His response was in continuity with the colonial forest policy, which defined the discouragement of shifting cultivation as integral to the political economy of conservation (premised on the view that a forest that did not generate revenue was wasteland). Thus, the recovery of wasteland required forestry programmes that would generate capital revenue. And so shifting cultivation was to be replaced with forestry. Thus, the State took over the forest and where it was possible, converted it into reserves of nature and displaced forest dwellers.

'Reserves of nature' included national parks, wildlife sanctuaries, and biosphere reserves. Amongst other features, they differed in terms of the nature of access given to the people. A large part of them was inaccessible to communities. The State has monopoly, that is, it has the sole right to decide who will look after it, and how it will be looked after. Community forests were demarcated for restricted human activity. These were distinct from forest plantations, which were used for commercial purposes. 'Reserves of nature', constructed by displacing people, can be conceptualised as manifestations of the contradiction between the rate of extraction and the rate of regeneration in nature.

One of the instruments with which to pursue this agenda to protect resources and make them available for industrial-commercial use across the world was linking conservation 'ex-situ', that is, 'off-site', away from the habitat of the plants, and 'in-situ', that is, on site, at the plants' habitat. Special attention was given to species classified as endangered and threatened. The strategy was to save the plants' genetic material in the laboratory and in nature reserves. The mandate was to conserve 'on-site' and extract the genetic material 'off-site' for industrial use.

This was a paradigm shift in the history conservation. Earlier, conservation had been associated with the uniqueness of nature and the focus was largely on landscapes, such as in the United States, United Kingdom, and Europe.[13] In India, conservation was inspired by the idea of non-violence and tolerance of other living beings, as in the case of Emperor Ashoka.[14] The establishment of reserves of nature changed the meaning of conservation to 'protective discrimination' and the selective use of natural resources. It anchored conservation on an industrial ground. Further, it sought to protect the forest from the less privileged people, adding one more layer to their social, political, and economic discrimination. The argument was that they could not look after the forest.

'Off-site' conservation in the laboratory was possible with biotechnologies, which depended on the information about 'plant use'. This information was available in the works of pioneering ethnobotanists, who had collected it from the indigenous people. In its early history, ethnobotany was concerned with listing the plants used by indigenous people. Field visits were planned for this purpose. Plant specimens were collected, their local/native name(s) recorded along with the Latin name, the geographical area(s) where the plant was found was identified, the plant population estimated, uses as told by informants (medicine men as well as frequent users) described. Further, they pressed and dried the plant and deposited it in an herbaria.

In 1896, the American botanist John Harshburger coined the term ethnobotany. Richard Evans Schultes, the father of ethnobotany, spent thirteen years in the Amazon (1941–1954) and returned to

Harvard University with 24,000 plant specimens, which are being studied today (Glenn 2005). Over the years, ethnobotanists studied plant folk taxonomy and learnt that indigenous plant knowledge is culturally embedded.

Claude Levi-Strauss investigated the classificatory aspects of the 'Savage Mind'. Quoting Smith Bowen, Levi-Strauss draws attention to the systematic knowledge of plants.

> ... Plants, like algebra, have a habit of looking alike and being different, or looking different and being alike.... I found myself in a place where every plant, wild or cultivated, had a name and a use and where every man, woman and child knew literally hundreds of plants.... [Levi-Strauss 1966 [1962], 6)
>
> ... Knowledge as systematically developed as this clearly cannot relate just to practical purposes.... (ibid., 8)
>
> The thought we call primitive is founded on this demand for order. This is equally true of all thought but it is through the properties common to all thought that we can most easily begin to understand forms of thought which seem very strange to us. (ibid., 10)

The development of biotechnology subverted and marginalised research of the cultural embeddedness of plants. Plant catalogues were used to serve corporate interests. A system of recording biodiversity in registers, known as biodiversity registers, was developed to help corporate interest. Typically, a corporate ethnobotanist will go to the field, make lists, undertake laboratory studies, and make the plant material available for economic industrial / commercial use.

For instance,

> In the field, ethnobotanists work as a team with an ethnomedicine-trained physician to prepare brief case descriptions of diseases. They then present these descriptions of individual diseases to shamans and the local healers, often including photographs of diseases with readily visible clinical manifestations. The interviewing process is conducted very carefully. The cases are presented without using medical terminology—terms such as herpes, hepatitis, or parasites are not necessarily understood by the local healers. The focus is on common signs and symptoms that are easily recognized. A translator for the local language is usually necessary to conduct

> this phase. Once a healer has recognized and described the same or similar disease state, the botanical treatment for that condition is recorded in detail by the ethnobotanist. If several independent and reliable shamans describe a similar treatment for a disease, the plant is collected.
>
> Additional plant collections and observations can also be made when Western trained physicians provide health care to the local people. The patient and the local healer are asked about the types of plants used to treat the disease state. Those plants that appear interesting are also collected for later analysis. (Veilleux, et al. n.d.)

The plant samples collected are taken to the laboratory and examined, where their active principles are identified. Thereafter, tests are conducted to verify the information regarding its medicinal properties listed by 'local informants'.

> Once the plants have arrived at the company's research site, processing the plants for medicinal purposes begins. The plants are tagged with the information from the field study. The plants are processed and tested in studies completed by ethnopharmacologists, using state of the art laboratory equipment (which may include High Pressure Liquid studies and in vivo transgenic animal studies). The objective is to screen the plants metabolites to determine how relevant they are to the therapeutic areas of interest. The most promising initial plant compounds are fractionated to obtain pure samples in milligram amounts. These natural pure compounds are compared to the best available therapeutics by in vitro testing. If the bioassay is successful, the compound is structurally characterized and is subject to a confirmatory biological test.
>
> Promising compounds are scaled up to provide gram quantities for animal testing to determine safety and efficacy. Pharmacologists with backgrounds in metabolism, pharmacokinetics, medicinal chemistry and formulation design experiments to determine whether the selected compounds have activity. After this testing is completed, the samples are compared with the best available marketed therapeutics. The scale up process occurs again and hundreds of grams of selected compounds are provided for further studies, which will, it is hoped, eventually lead to an effective, marketable drug suitable for human consumption. This new product is the reward for all the time and effort of many individuals. (Veilleux, et al. n.d.)

This search for knowledge about the properties of forest materials is based on the observation that their use of plants can offer strong clues to biological activity.

It is clear that the sustainability of industrial production based on forest materials, especially of food grains and medicine, is not possible without 'reserves of nature'. They contribute billions of dollars yearly to the world economy in the form of improved crop species, new drugs and medicines, and raw materials for industry.[15]

At the same time,

> Knowledge about the world's life forms lags surprisingly behind other fields of scientific enquiry. While a great deal is known about individual species of birds, fishes, mammals, and plants, fewer than 1.4 million of the world's 5–30 million species have been named, let alone studied in detail. Knowledge about the structure and functioning of ecosystems is just as scant.
>
> Information is also limited on the conditions and value of biological resources, as well as uses and management techniques employed by traditional cultures over the centuries. (World Resources. 1992–1993, 134–135)

This raises questions. Do reserves of nature facilitate conservation? Is biodiversity less vulnerable than when indigenous people lived in the forest? In what way do reserves contribute to science, specifically to overcoming the scantiness of the knowledge in this field? The knowledge of forest dwellers is valued, but their way of life that generates this knowledge and where this knowledge is embedded is not valued. Why?

From public debates, we know that nature is vulnerable after the creation of 'reserves'. For instance, the tiger population has dwindled drastically. There is pressure on these reserves from people on the margins; as destructive development adds more people to the army of cheap labour, the prospects of controlling poaching are not in sight because the officialdom in charge of the reserves is hand-in-glove with the poachers. Further, the legal regime and the system of governance for these reserves are fragmented on account of an inter-departmental lack of coordination and cooperation. Most important is the absence of people who are comfortable being in the forest. Most of the staff on duty to look after the forests has no love for it. They perceive their job as no less than a punishment post.[16]

The problem lies in the way the forest is thought about. Regulatory regimes for 'reserves of nature' are defined by a theory of ecology that places the tiger at the apex. A typical regulatory regime is an arrangement in concentric circles. For instance, a biosphere reserve has a core area that is the interior-most, after which lies the buffer area, and then the outermost concentric circle, which is the periphery. This mode is centralised and its patriarchal totem is the tiger.

As regards the second question—the making of reserves of nature does not contribute to knowledge about biodiversity—the views of the community of scientists are as follows.

> .... evidence from Amazonian natives suggests that indigenous knowledge of medicinal plants can develop over a relatively short period of time.
>
> Ethnobotanists studying medicinal plant use by recently contacted tribes like the Waorani of Ecuador and the Yanomani of Brazil and Venezuela reported a relatively limited and highly selective use of medicinal plants.... Their repertoire did not include plants to treat any Western diseases. In contrast, indigenous groups that have had a history of continuing contact with the outside world have hundreds of medicinal plants used for a wide range of conditions. It seems that after contact, in response to the introduction of Western diseases, these tribes accelerated their experimentation with medicinal plants. This notion contradicts the idea that indigenous knowledge of medicinal plants was accumulated slowly.... (Butler 2005)

As forest dwellers enter the mainstream, they lose not only this knowledge but also the method of discovery. This is a big loss. What labour went into the discovery of this knowledge? How did they know the medicinal and other related properties of plants? What did they observe? How and where did they record their observations, study them, and pass on the results of their study to the next generation?

These questions are not important for the corporate ethnobotanist who works with biotechnologies, for their equipment works on what has already been discovered. The touch of plants in their field settings (ex-situ) does not inspire the nature and scope of their research;

instead, motivation is related to the demands of industry and the tradition of mainstream scientific botany, which is increasingly becoming less of a science and more of a technological outpost—that of economic botany.

The 'Intellectual Property Rights' regime is not concerned with the interdependence of 'in-situ' and 'ex-situ' conservation; this is premised on the interdependence of the 'laboratory' and the 'reserves of nature'. The indigenous work and process of discovery are ignored because there is no theoretical value of the labor that goes into discovery. Indigenous discovery is dismissed as 'hit and trial'. It is clear that the techno-science theoretical frame determines the use (application) of this knowledge, but does not recognise and delegitimises any attempt to inquire into the how of indigenous discovery.

The awareness that the knowledge of plants is culturally embedded has not prepared the ground for collaborative work between corporate ethnobotany, the indigenous medicine men, and pharmaceutical companies. Such a collaboration is premised on the view that the forest is biomass-rich and abundant with biodiversity, all of which is interconnected in an arrangement of a network of food webs, food chains, and ecological niches. Here, the forest is an entity without a being, that is to say, it exists in parts. This is demonstrated in the fact that all conservation is largely species-specific.

This view lacks the perception that the universe of the forest is a living space—a home and a place of work. For this reason, the relation with the forest is unilateral and the relation to nature non-reciprocal. This can enable nothing other than the extraction of raw materials from nature, without giving it time for rest, recuperation, and regeneration.

Indigenousness and Conservation

The Native American people and the forest dwellers in India and in other parts of the world first made the effort to transform natural landscapes into social-cultural spaces for human settlement. The time, the physical energy, and the intellectual work that constituted this effort were immense, spread over several generations. We know only the products of this labor, but have very little understanding of the processes and methods that constituted such labor. The indigenous refers to this labor as that which determines the grounded-ness of a people to a place. Such grounded-ness is at the core of a sense of belonging. In other words, 'I belong where my labor grounds me'.

The indigenous thus stands opposed to everything that undermines the value of the labor that grounds people and a way of life. The cultural embeddedness suggests that indigenous knowledge is grounded in a way of life shaped by phenomena in plural universes of nature, as we know of them from the touch of the forest, of the sea, of the hills and mountains, and not the abstracted nature as we see under a microscope.

Indigenous conservation is based on nature's presentation of its own activity.[17] The readiness or the preparedness to receive the way nature 'presents its own being' is at the core of the indigenous methodology of conservation. How do we know that 'nature presents its own being'? By what means do we know this? Why is this important?

A pre-requisite to investigating these questions is to be comfortable in a forest, and observe, know, and look after it. Those who think the forest is uncomfortable, move in jeeps on forest roads. They cannot be caretakers. The forest is most vulnerable under the surveillance of forest guards who move by jeeps, and who can barely walk the depth of the forest.

What does it require to be comfortable in the forest? It is to be at home when lost in it, to not panic and make the effort to recover a sense of direction, and participate in the soundscapes—differentiate and recognise the sources of sounds. When lost in the forest, we are in a position to see the universe of the forest in the way it presents itself. The recovery of one's position is not possible without seeing and feeling how the forest presents itself. This is crucial to discovering the forest.[18]

An example of participating in the soundscapes will illustrate the idea of reciprocity.

> Cordova-Rios, a Peruvian doctor was captured in 1907, when he was fifteen years old, by a small tribe of Amahuaca Indians living deep in the Amazon rain forest.... He was carefully trained by the

> headman of the tribe to become his successor, and was for six years meticulously tutored in the ways of the hunt, in the medicinal and magical powers of the rain forest plants. The tribe's language, which remained largely meaningless for more than six months, became understandable to his ears only as his senses became attuned to the rain forest ecology in which the culture was embedded ... his description of the various hunts in which he participated make it vividly evident the extent to which these people's senses were directly coupled to the enveloping forest.... They reacted to the faintest signals of sound and smell, intuitively relating them to all other conditions of the environment and then interpreting them to achieve the greatest possible capture of the game.... (Abram 1997, 141–142)

The *siraha* or *guniya* (shaman) illustrates one way of getting lost in the forest. Often, they walk into the forest and do not return for several days. Members of their families know that this is a call of the forest. They may not return at all. Where they go and what they do to live, no one can tell. On their return, they sometimes tell stories of where they went and what they saw. Often they keep quiet.

Both these examples suggest that the way to learn to receive nature as it presents itself on its own (and becomes accessible for us to receive) is to be ready to hand over one's self to nature. There is a suggestion here of a way to not exercise one's will, to restrain and undo the necessity for a presentation of the self. This is a preparation to listen. In the act of listening, we are able to receive the forest soundscape, for listening is possible only when one's self is ready to receive. By means of such reciprocity, the forest reveals itself in its rhythms. Often, my Koitor friends drew my attention to sounds, which I could not hear because I was preoccupied with my-self and was thus not making myself available.

Long stays in the forest make it possible to flow along the rhythm of the day, the week, the month, the season, and the year. It is no slower or faster than the rhythm of the sun and the moon. The relation between rhythm, reciprocity, and seeing can be illustrated from the way we see a tree. To be able to see life on a tree, it is necessary to not move faster than the tree. One needs to learn to be as grounded, be as still as the tree and be attuned to its rhythm. This is reciprocal seeing. Why is it not possible to make the effort to become like a tree in order to know the tree?

What we see and what we 'can' see is a function of the rate at which we cover distance—our speed. This is not possible using a frame for it freezes a moment, which is in contradiction with the fact that all things that constitute our life-world are in continuous movement. The frozen moment then needs to be interpreted, imaginatively, before and after it is constructed. A metaphor of the frame is 'lens', it is either convex or concave and it distorts. This frame cannot be used to see and observe.

Seeing is reciprocal. The observer and the observed see each other, and this is possible only under certain conditions, when both are mutually accessible. Their relative positioning in time and space is therefore important. A fast-moving object cannot see one that is slower, and vice versa. The greater the difference of speed between the two, the less they can see each other. However, 'the space' in which the movement happens is better viewed by the slower object than by the faster one. Seeing is thus possible when the observer and the observed are available to each other in time and space.

Lens frames what is being observed (we may refer to it as body) and in the process alienates the framed part from the rest of the body and also from the observer. The framed part is thus rendered passive. In contrast, in reciprocal seeing the observer is also the observed as much as the observed is the observer; both are actively responding to each other. This is more than inter-subjectivity; it is a mode of being in resonance, as it were. For this reason, reciprocity is not possible without listening and restraint—that is, to not impose a view or perception. To give time and space to what is being observed is to present it. To be restrained is a way of becoming prepared to receive.

Reciprocal seeing exists not only between human beings, but also between hills, rivers, plants, animals, and human beings. The universe of the forest is thus a set of conditions that contribute to such seeing and the creation of knowledge. Care is of crucial importance to this. To understand this phenomenon, we could reflect on what Ramchandra Gandhi points out, namely that forest is '*aranya*', literally 'that which cannot be battled'. It is a metaphor of self, a promise, and a place of peace (Gandhi 2005, 28). Who can be 'that which cannot be battled'? What are its attributes? Such a being cannot be conceptualised as invincible, for the expression 'invincible' already assumes going into battle in order to establish invincibility. In my view, the term describes what the forest evokes in anyone who is in a reciprocal relation with it—a sense of warmth and care. It presents itself as a sheltering space with immense capacity to rejuvenate and heal on its own. Does this not make it 'that which cannot be battled'? I think it does, because it exists in a mode that is its own and interdependent. To be that which cannot be battled is also a mode of being in the world.

The ecology and praxis of conservation grounded in the notion 'aranya' has at least five attributes that correspond to the attributes of 'that which cannot be battled'. These are: plurality; judiciousness; resilience; wholeness; and sheltering.

The plurality of the forest is manifest in the soundscape and camouflage. Both describe abundance and diversity of life forms. Plurality is different from multiplicity. In plurality, there is an abundance of different kinds. In multiplicity there is abundance of one kind—as in multiples of one. In plurality there is freedom and interdependence, there is a sense of being self-contained and interrelated, and there is thus the possibility of existence in symbiosis and synergy. It regulates excesses (for instance, the population ratios). That is to say, it restrains any one living form from multiplying at the expense of other living forms. Plurality of species is thus necessary for the constitution of a food chain.

The Koitors describe it as Shringarbhum—a decorated landscape. Here, mother earth is judicious. In its universe there is abundance and variety; there is camouflage for fluid boundaries, which shelters self-containment alongside interrelation. A landscape rich with 'abundant variety' needs a special kind of space demarcation—one that enables inter-spatiality. This is provided by camouflage. That is to say, a space is shared by different species. There is no exclusive prerogative over the space of any one species at the expense of others. For example, two tigers or two monkeys will fight over their territory, but they live in a space where a variety of species abound. Further, when species migrate from one place to another, they relinquish their territorial prerogative. Thus, there are no immutable monopolies, and no ghettoisation. This inter-spatiality across species is the ground for processes of continuous regeneration and seamlessness, without any dissipation of energy or waste. The symbiosis, food chains, and ecological cycles of plants and animals utilise everything; such is mother earth's economy of nature. Without camouflage, there will be a need for barriers in the likeness of a zoo.

Resilience is the capacity to remain grounded; withstand the wear and tear of time; heal and recover from illness; and when 'lost', restore the pathway for well-being. All these go towards making a dwelling. The forest has an inner strength to stand up to the heat from the sun, contain monsoon water from flooding, break the speed of strong winds, and provide food when the earth retires to rest. It has the plurality of living beings to resist illness and its capacity for regeneration ensures a quick recovery.

In restraint there is wholeness, the possibility of seamless interconnectedness. Restraint in speech, movement, and occupation of space makes available time and space to others, without which it is not possible to see, and to be free and self-reliant. The universe of the forest conditions living beings to not take more than their share, leaving enough for others. What is there for taking is the product of one's own labor. In other words, labor restrains us to not take that which is not invested with one's own labor—this is the realm of 'work of nature'. This is the principle of restraint. This is the ground for the inter-spatiality of species described above.

Sheltering is a mode of being in the world, in the likeness of trees. Trees ground life processes. They regulate the height of the canopy, the play of heat and light shades, and the flow of reserves of water. The variation in height, in the girth and texture of the trunk, in the lateral spread, in the shape and the width of leaves, in the depth of the roots ensure recovery and restoration. The tree heals by giving shelter in reciprocity to those who care for it. In a similar way, to shelter is to be grounded, give warmth, and heal. These five attributes that we learn from the forest are key components of the ecology and praxis of conservation.

The Brief

The intention of radical assertion and an insistence on care as a way of being in the world is to explore the vicissitudes of hope at the limits of human existence. Such is the way of indigenous caretakers. The brief of indigenousness, thus, is to break the vicious circle of deforestations—the production and reproduction of tools; processes and structures of violence and mass destruction; the colonisation of the self by the self; and a reduction in the capacity to regenerate, recover from injury, and rejuvenate.

The praxis of conservation is concerned with what constitutes justice.

Endnotes

1. Fieldwork in Bastar, Jharkhand.

2. For a discussion on this binary opposition, see Briggs (2005, 1).

3. See Kingsbury (1998) for a detailed account of the overlaps, convergences, and differences.

4. Several terms have emerged to refer to indigenous people—autochthonous, ethnic minorities, tribal people, First Nation, Fourth World—which seek to emphasise their distinctiveness from the dominant mainstream.

5. '[W]hose social and economic conditions are at a less advanced stage than ... other sections of the national community, and whose status regulated wholly or partially by their own customs or traditions or by special laws or regulations; as well as those "which are regarded as indigenous on account of their descent from the population which inhabited the country ... at the time of conquest and which live more in conformity with the social, economic and cultural institutions of that time than with [national] institutions"' (Barsh 1987, 757).

6. 'For the past few years, increasing concern has been expressed at various international forums over the problem of the loss of cultural identity among the Indian populations of Latin America. This complex process, which has historical, social, political and economic roots, has been termed ethnocide.

Ethnocide means that an ethnic group is denied the right to enjoy, develop and transmit its own culture and its own language, whether collectively or individually. This involves an extreme form of massive violation of human rights and, in particular, the right of ethnic groups to respect for their cultural identity, as established by numerous declarations, covenants and agreements of the United Nations and its Specialized Agencies, as well as various regional intergovernmental bodies and numerous nongovernmental organizations.

Organizations representing various indigenous groups in Latin America and experts in the field have proclaimed, with growing insistence, the need to counter ethnocide and to set in motion an authentic process of ethno-development, that is, the establishment and application of policies guaranteeing ethnic groups the free enjoyment of their own cultures.

In response to this demand, UNESCO organized an international meeting on ethnocide and ethno-development in Latin America, in collaboration with FLACSO, which was held in December 1981 in San Jose.' (UNESCO 1981, 1).

7. See Barsh (1987) for discussions that contributed to the making of the ILO Convention 169.

8. ILO Convention 169, Article 1 and 7, respectively.

9. For instance, UNESCO organised a 'Meeting of Experts' on the study of ethno-development and ethnocide in Europe. In a document whose circulation was limited, extracts from a study of Gypsies in Europe were shared. See de Gila-Kochanowski (1983).

The consequences of World Wars I and II played an important role in the formulation and acceptance of this declaration. On the one hand, the UN inherited a series of political instruments signed after the Wars. These contained special measures for the protection of ethnic, religious, and linguistic groups, and referred to minorities in Poland, Austria, the Serbo–Croat–Slovenic State, Czechoslovakia, Bulgaria, Romania, Hungary, Albania, Lithuania, Greece, Turkey, Estonia, and Iraq, amongst others. On the other hand, the sordid story of Nazi genocide made it more than clear that all genocide begins with cultural aggression.

10. Some interesting essays on this subject can be found in Barsh (1986); Swepston (1989); and Wright (1988).

11. Similarly, the epic of the Kutti Khonda in Phulbani also describes the process of making a forest one's living place.

12. This is different from common pool resources or common property resources, both of which are derivatives of the notion of property.

13. The history of the idea of such reserves can be traced to the suggestion for national parks given by William Wordsworth in 1880, when he described the Lake District in the UK as the sort of national property to which 'every man has a right and interest who has the eye to perceive and a heart to enjoy'. Similarly, the painter George Catlin, in his travels through

the American West, wrote in 1832 that the Native Americans in the United States 'might be preserved by some great protecting policy of the government ... in a magnificent park....'

The first government effort to set aside such protected land was in the United States, when President Abraham Lincoln signed the Act of Congress on 30 June 1864, ceding Yosemite Valley and the Mariposa Grove of Giant Sequoias (which later became the Yosemite National Park) to the State of California. In 1872, the Yellowstone National Park was established as the first truly national park. Following it there were several parks in other nations: the Royal National Park in Australia, south of Sydney (1879), and the Banff National Park, Canada (1887). In Europe, the first set of nine parks were established in Sweden in 1910. After World War II, national parks were founded all over the world. See http://en.wikipedia.org/wiki/National_park (accessed May 2023).

14. It is said that in India, conservation was inspired by the ideas of non-violence and tolerance of other living beings, as demonstrated by Emperor Ashoka who, in 200 BC, made the first wildlife conservation law. See https://forest.mizoram.gov.in/uploads/attachments/84baecdbb7b57161c1344182a059b16d/pages-163-2-the-wild-life-protection-act-1972.pdf (accessed June 2023).

15. In 1983, there were no pharmaceutical firms from the United States involved in the research on such plants, while today, well over 100 companies and government agencies are pursuing the study of rainforest plants for their medicinal potential (Butler 2005).

16. Based on my fieldwork.

17. Except where I quote, the discussion that follows is based on long fieldwork in the forest.

18. Based on my fieldwork in Abujhmarh and Similipal.

six

Contemplating Social Justice*

It is worth considering that a notion of justice determined by the presence of the forest universe is meaningful for social life as such. This notion of justice is concerned with the injustices that stem from the 'denial of language and not listening'. This chapter underlines the hermeneutic injustice consequent to the denial of one's own language to uphold value generated either from utility or from scarcity, or from the objectification of subjectivity.

From the Koitors, we learn that in the presence of the universe of the forest, justice lies in recognising that everything that comes to be part of landscapes must also, of necessity, dissolve back into it. Correspondingly, things come to be when remembered, and dissolve when forgotten. Both are of equal importance and must happen. Here, reflexivity, an attribute of critical thinking, is nourished by both memory and forgetting when confronted with the question: What is worthy of memory and what is worthy of forgetting?

Koitors have no reluctance in learning a new language. When they communicate with speakers of other language(s), they maintain their own language and the different languages complement each other. This is because they know that no one single language can fulfil *all* the functions of everyday communication.

Language holds memory and different languages remember differently. Equally, a loss of language induces forgetting (a loss of

*An earlier version of this chapter was published as 'With the Gaze on Injustice Positioning the Tribal People in the Wider Social Context', in *Journal of the National Human Rights Commission of India* 15, 2016.

memory). To forget everything and to not forget anything both undermine social well-being. Accordingly, from this perspective, justice is respectful of this association of language and memory.

The fetishising of memory (to try to hold on to every thing, occurrence, experience) and forced forgetting (wishing it away) are both unjust. To hold on, not letting them pass away (dissolve) is to privilege remembering, and equally, to wish things away (force them out of memory) is to privilege forgetting. Such injustice is perpetuated when critical thinking entangled in the fetishised memory does not listen to those who do not abide by its norm, and respect diverse ways of exploring and knowing the relation between knowledge and way of life, thereby effectively forcing these other ways out of historical memory.

Thus, the 'right to one's language (its modes of memory alongside forgetting) and [to] be heard in it' is a principle of justice that flows from deference to the diverse relations between knowledge and way of life. When no such deference exists, then either there is no one listening, or there is a pretence to listening, or there is cacophony because everyone is speaking and no one is listening. Correspondingly, the injustice of 'not being heard' occurs when people are made to give up their own language and acquire the language of others who are in a dominating position. On account of this structural prejudice in the economy of hermeneutics, all languages of everyday communications lose credibility. Here, value is generated either from utility or from scarcity, or from the objectification of subjective value.

This gives rise to what Miranda Fricker (2007) describes as testimonial injustice and hermeneutical injustice.

> Testimonial injustice occurs when (*prejudice*) causes a hearer to give a deflated level of credibility to a speaker's word; hermeneutical injustice occurs ..., when a gap in collective interpretive resources (*created on account of using one language to fulfill all functions*) puts someone at an unfair disadvantage when it comes to making sense of their social experiences. An example of the first might be that the police do not believe you because you are black; an example of the second might be that you suffer sexual harassment in a culture that still lacks that critical concept. We might say that testimonial

> injustice is caused by prejudice in the economy of credibility; and that hermeneutical injustice is caused by structural prejudice in the economy of collective hermeneutical resources. The overarching aim is to bring to light certain ethical aspects of two of our most basic everyday epistemic practices: conveying knowledge to others by telling them, and making sense of our own social experiences. (ibid., 1; emphasis mine)

Testimonial and hermeneutic injustice are violations, either by imposing upon or through replacing (by force or through educational institutions) the language of an individual and a group with a foreign language, or by looking down upon the civil conventions to learn each other's language in the course of everyday interactions. This chapter presents a documentation of this injustice with regard to the tribal people of India.

The Linguistic Survey of India, undertaken towards the latter part of the insurgency period 1783–1900, recorded 179 languages and 544 dialects. Of the 179 languages, 116 were enumerated as tribal languages and dialects. This survey was begun in 1898 by an Irish linguistic scholar and civil servant, Sir George Abraham Grierson (1851–1941), with support from the International Congress of Orientologists held in Vienna in 1886. The survey was completed in 1928, after thirty years. Grierson (2001) observed, 'It was noted that it was rare for one Indo-Aryan language to be replaced by another Indo-Aryan language. It was very often the case that a local tribal language was replaced by an Indo-Aryan language.'

Grigson suggested that this was on account of cognitive regulation and control,

> In most of India aboriginal pressure groups are still unthinkable, for there has been no political education of the aboriginal. Political democracy, working through legislatures and local bodies created by direct election, is almost meaningless to him; hardly anyone has dreamt of 'economic democracy' and training for a democratic way of life, for instance through aboriginal co-operatives.
>
> Our immediate objectives should therefore, I think, be threefold: (a) to keep Indian thought increasingly aware of the aboriginal problem as its own 'colonial' problem and 'on its honor' to solve it; (b)

> to take stock of the economic, cultural, political, administrative and anthropological material and gauge what further enquiry is needed; and (c) to attempt to define for the new governments in India the aims to be pursued in their treatment of the tribes. (Grigson 1944, 37–38)

The work of G. S. Ghurye and Verrier Elwin contributed to cognitive regulation and control. Ghurye positioned tribal people within the caste system.

> With the exception of very small sections living in 'the recesses of hills and the depths of forests', the so-called aboriginals, sharing common interests in matters of faith and livelihood, had lived in 'fairly intimate contact with Hindus over a long time'. The sociologist concluded that the 'only proper description of these people' is that they are 'the imperfectly integrated classes of Hindu society'. Hence his own preference for the term 'backward Hindu' instead of 'aborigine' or 'aboriginal'. (Ghurye, quoted in Guha 1996, 2385)

Elwin also positioned tribals in the caste system. In 1944, he wrote,

> Missionaries should be withdrawn from the Partially Excluded areas; we insist that all education in these areas should be taken over by the Government.... We have no interest in keeping these people backward. If they are to take their place as Kshatriyas in the Hindu social system then they must be trained in the arts of liberal thinking and educated to courage and traditions of honor. (Prasad 2003, 91–92)

What came of these suggestions? The Survey of the Peoples of India, undertaken in the 1980s under the guidance of the late K. Suresh Singh, Director-General of the Anthropological Survey of India, identified 4,635 communities in India, of which 461 were tribal. Amongst other things, it reported the peoples' awareness of their caste identity.

> About 31.6 per cent of tribes were found to be aware of the varna system and 16.7 per cent placed themselves within it: nearly 8.3 per cent claimed to be Kshatriya; 7.5 per cent thought that they were Shudra; and 0.9 per cent placed themselves in the high caste varna

> of Brahmin. Gaddi Brahmin, Pangwal Brahmin, Kagati, and some among the Jaunsari claimed to be Brahmin. The Pardhan (of Madhya Pradesh) called themselves Vaishya.... 171 tribes (26.9 per cent) that thought they were of a high status; 298 (46.9 per cent) that perceived themselves as being in a middle position; and 161 (25.3 per cent) that saw themselves as being of low status. These self-perceptions were however not uncontested. (Srivastava 2010, 11)

This awareness introduced a disjunction between people's languages and their way of life in the universe of the forest. This disjunction was deepened when the Constituent Assembly (1949–1950) included the partially excluded and excluded areas under the Fifth and Sixth Schedules of the Constitution, without a discussion on tribal language. In 2000, it was reported,

> By going through the deliberations in the Constituent Assembly and the Indian Parliament, it becomes clear that neither the Constituent Assembly nor the Indian Parliament debated the language question of the country as a whole. What has been debated is whether English or Hindi would be the National Official Languages and what role Sanskrit should play in the scheme of languages. Jawaharlal Nehru's recommendation for the use and protection of tribal languages fell on deaf ears. (Rani 2000, 415)

What was the impact of these Schedules? The dominant ethnic groups continued to give preference to non-tribal languages in public places, consequently discouraging the use of their mother tongues. The tribals were compelled to recognise and learn non-tribal languages for inter-group communication, as well as for social mobility, economic emancipation, and status. Over time, the tribals began to identify themselves with the majority language of their area (Rani 2000, 416). Without this, it would not be possible to mainstream.

This, however, contributed to illiteracy. In 2014, the Xaxa Committee reported an increase in illiteracy alongside mainstreaming. With regard to mainstreaming, it says,

> The triumphs of and shortcomings of mainstreaming are reported over a wide range of subjects. These include the role of public policy

> and legal frameworks, geographical pattern of economic activity; changes in avenues of employment and livelihood due to rapid urbanization and shrinking of habitat; relative share of public and private employment; changes in the patterns of ownership; access to educational and health services, level of literacy and dropout rates; maternal and infant mortality rate; level of social infrastructure.... (Government of India 2014)

As regards illiteracy, it says,

> Most of the tribal communities in India have their own mother tongue. But in most of the States, official/regional languages are used for classroom teaching and these are not understood by the tribal children at primary level of schooling. In the Vision 2020 document, there was an acknowledgement that Multi-Lingual Education (MLE) was necessary, in view of the low tribal literacy, high rates of dropouts and low learning achievements of the tribal children. The Model of Primers in the Tribal language was first developed in Odisha in 1996. Subsequently, several pilot projects involving material production and training, aimed at promoting multilingualism in the classrooms were launched in Odisha, Andhra Pradesh and Assam.
>
> The design of the Primer of Odisha has some aspects, which should be noted for replication. One side of the text was in local script but used tribal language. The other side of the script was in local language and script. The student learnt the script because he/she understood the content. The teacher understood the tribal language because he/she could read in a known script. The contents were about local trees and fruits, local folk tales and festivals. Some of the text was also about functional literacy such as clean drinking water and common institutions. However, this initiative was not carried forward with change of personnel at the helm of Education Departments. (Government of India 2014, 184)

Why did incentives not work to increase enrolment and attendance, get good teachers, and reduce dropout rates? The Xaxa Committee does not address this question. Neither does it dwell on the correlation of illiteracy and mainstreaming. A language barrier does not explain illiteracy. There is more to it.

To discuss this question, it is necessary to recognise that the tribal conversions to Hinduism and Christianity were accompanied by the loss of language. It is Christians and Hindus who have predominantly sought to convert tribal people.

> .... Almost 100 per cent of respondents to the Census of India, 2001, gave a religious affiliation ... 0.6 per cent were Other Religions, which includes the 'tribal religions and faiths'.
>
> Christianity had spread remarkably among the tribes of north-east India, in Manipur (94.55 per cent), Nagaland (93.09 per cent), Mizoram (88.46 per cent), and Meghalaya (66.32 per cent). There had also been a rise in the number of tribal followers of Christianity in Bihar (11.87 per cent), Kerala (5.62 per cent), and Tripura (3.95 per cent). (Srivastava 2010, 11–12)

Hindu tribals are found in larger proportions: ' ... in Gujarat 97.8 per cent of tribals profess Hinduism, 1.7 per cent are Christians and 0.2 per cent are Muslim. In addition, there are 2,166 Jains, 390 Sikhs, 231 Buddhists, and 11,678 tribespersons belonging to Other Religions and Persuasions' (Srivastava 2010, 11–12).

There is, however, a wide range of variations.

> Some tribes follow only one religion. However, in many there are followers of more than one religion, such as Hinduism and tribal religion (90 tribes, 21 per cent), Christianity and tribal religion (55 tribes, 13 per cent), or, more commonly, Hinduism, Islam, and Christianity. The survey was able to discern the following three trends, which are still continuing. (ibid., 11)
>
> In many tribes, particularly the larger ones, different sections follow different religions; thus, for example, over half the Oraon are Hindu (58.43 per cent of the total population) and a fifth are Christian (21.05 per cent), with a minuscule proportion (around 0.04 per cent) following Islam, Sikhism or Buddhism. (ibid., 10)

Conversions endeavoured to replace the symbolic universe of the people. This gradually marginalised the expressions of tribal languages, making them extraneous and irrelevant. This is one factor that led to the loss of these languages.

> More than eighty years back, George Grierson undertook the Linguistic Survey of India in 1927. At that time he mentioned about 179 languages and 544 dialects. Subsequently, the 1931 Census, the last enumeration done by the British, listed more than 2000 languages....
>
> However, there is no denying the fact that the tribal languages were forced into a corner. Not a single language of vast tribal people in India had been accorded official status till 2004. Only Santhali language has been recognized very recently. Tribal languages like Gondi, Oraon/Kurukh with more than millions of speakers are not yet scheduled in the Constitution of India. Historically and culturally, the tribal people in India and Orissa in particular have been playing important roles. Some of these tribal languages have more numerical strength than some of those mentioned in the Eighth Schedule of the Constitution. For instance, besides Santhali, the number of speakers of Gondi and Oraon/Kurukh languages is more than the speakers of Sanskrit and Kashmiri and Sindhi. (Pasayat 2008, 63–65)

Furthermore, the UNESCO Atlas of World Endangered Languages

> ... identifies 196 languages that are endangered in India, which comprise 84 languages that are 'unsafe', 62 languages that are 'definitely endangered' and six and 33 languages that are respectively 'severely' and 'critically' endangered (Table 2). Nine languages—Ahom, Aimol, Andro, Chairel, Kolhreng, Rangkas, Sengmai, Tarao and Tolcha—have become extinct in India from the 1950s. Though these endangered languages are spread across the entire country there is some degree of concentration, with many of these languages being located in the Northeast as well as the tribal belts of West Bengal and Orissa and in Himachal Pradesh, Jammu and Kashmir and Uttarakhand. These languages are also diverse in terms of the number of speakers, who range from zero to 27.14 lakhs (Gondi) as per the 2001 Census.... (Sengupta 2009, 18)

This is only the tip of the iceberg. A more detailed and nuanced study of the status of tribal languages is necessary.

When there is a loss of the symbolic universe alongside the loss of language, then people's epistemological and ontological imagination is undermined. This isolation deprived people of the space to respond to representations that belittled, demeaned, and destroyed their pride in their culture. The popular stereotypes that continue to be hurled are 'the lazy native', 'perpetually drunk', with 'lose sexual behaviour' and 'inhuman cultural practices'.

Tribal languages were looked down upon because they lacked a written script on the one hand, and because they were seen as being embedded in traditions and ways of life that were considered inferior, and for this reason were to be replaced, on the other.

> Writing about 'Aliens in their own home' Sudhir Shukla (*The Hindu*, March 14, 1993) writes, On his first day in a remote village school in Madhya Pradesh, six year old Bishnoo asks his friend Surta to 'Ingey Vaita' (Gondi for 'Come here'). But what follows is a scream from the teacher. 'Chup baith, janwar kahin ka' (Shut up, you village idiot). Shukla further writes, 'cowed down, little Bishnoo does not know whether he was wrong in using Gondi in the classroom which has invited his teacher's wrath. But within few months he learns that speaking his native tongue in the classroom is an offense. Though Bishnoo cannot understand the Hindi of the teacher or of the text books he realises that the only language he knows has no place in the school'. (Rani 2000, 417)

One important reason for the low prestige accorded to tribal languages, as mentioned earlier, is the absence of a written script.

> ... As a matter of fact, Indian civilisation has found its expression primarily through the Aryan speech as it developed through the centuries.... After the Aryan speech, Dravidian has also very largely functioned as the exponent of Indian culture—particularly the earlier secular as well as religious literature of Tamil, which has some special characteristics of its own within the Indian orbit....
>
> All the other languages were in a backward state, as the speakers of these were in a comparatively primitive condition in their way of life. Of course, they had some kind of village or folk culture, but no civilisation. Connected with this culture there developed in all these languages a slight modicum of folk-literature—of songs, religious and otherwise, of folk-tales, and of their legends and traditions. These were never written down as they lacked any system of writing.... (Chatterjee 1971, 6)

This low prestige associated with tribal languages has legitimised linguistic acculturation for mainstreaming. This leads to linguistic suicide and extinction. Linguistic suicide occurs when an 'older generation of speakers dominant in the minority language deliberately choose not to teach this language to their children and adopts a majority language as the language of child rearing, thereby willfully interrupting the transmission of their language to the next generation' (Beck and Yvonne n.d., 27).

In India, linguistic suicide occurred with conversion. As regards conversion, we know that Christian missionaries under the colonial regimes used these so-called 'other languages' to replace their speakers' worldview with the Christian one.

> A serious study of these ... began only during the middle of the 19th century when European scholars—anthropologists and linguists—as well as European Christian missionaries of various denominations (like Roman Catholics from Belgium, France, Germany, Italy, Spain, England and Ireland, German Lutherans, Scandinavian Lutherans, English Anglicans, Scottish Presbyterians, and Welsh Methodists) began to study these languages and take in hand the preparation of a Christian literature (both of translations from the Bible and other Christian sacred literature, and of original compositions to a small extent) for the purpose of converting these backward peoples into Christianity. They succeeded in doing this to a very large extent as these peoples were neglected by the Hindu ruling classes who had contact with them. (Chatterjee 1971, 6–7)

Conversion to Christianity was initiated through medical care and prayer services. Missionaries were not always trained doctors; however, even with rudimentary medicines and healthcare, they were able to cure people. Their success earned them credibility and the necessary ground to bring people for prayer services. According to the missionaries, tribal people would accept Christianity with little difficulty because, unlike the Hindus and Muslims, tribal people had no dogmatic theology. In postcolonial India, in reaction to the Christians, conversion to Hinduism, which was already underway, became aggressive. They too initiated processes for imitating rituals and ceremonies. In development programmes tribal people were used for their labour power, and the tasks given to them required minimal use of their mother tongues. In schools established by Christians and later by the State, tribal language was not a medium of instruction. In fact, tribal students continue to be discouraged from speaking in their mother tongue.

As a result, for the people, their language became associated with economic exclusion from mainstream societies. The social, cultural, economic, political, and psychological pressures generated here contributed to the development of a disapproving and unconstructive attitude towards their language. It led speakers to doubt the usefulness of their language in the business of everyday life. Amongst other things, this inhibited the transmission of language. It has been observed that speakers of minority languages deliberately choose not to use their language when communicating with their children; instead, they adopt a majority language, thereby deliberately interrupting the transmission of their language to the next generation and reducing the social domains in which the language can be used. Here, tribal language is used to recast the terms by communicating the inferiority of the culture to the tribal people themselves, and legitimising mimesis, that is, imitating the habits of eating, dressing, sitting, customary religious rituals, and codes of conduct of mainstream culture.

Conversions in Bihar, Jharkhand, and Odisha have become the basis for the exchange of hostilities between Christians and Hindus. It has similarly impacted the tribal people inhabiting the Northeast region. The rest of the nation only knows of these people through demeaning racist stereotypes that pick on their physical features and eating habits. Here, the divide is not between the 'red' and the 'monochromatic' corridor. In its place is an absolute military presence, overlaid with comprehensive Christian conversion. This military presence has isolated and suffocated the living traditions from the wider social context, allowing little space and time for people to speak up using expressions of their own language.

Irom Sharmila's long years of fasting have drawn attention to the 'frontier' of the Northeast. It critiques the perception of 'frontier', where there is an 'absolute presence of the military'. Her fasting was an appeal to the diverse people of the Northeast engaged in conflicts to recognise persuasion as a cultural mode to prevent conflict from spreading in the lives of the people in this region. It was also an appeal to the State to free the people from suffocation on account of the Armed Forces Special Powers Act (AFSPA) and have trust in the people's capacity to look after themselves and the region.

I saw a glimpse of the cultural manifestations of linguistic suicide in the course of working with the Koitors of Shringarbhum, Bastar, Chhattisgarh, and the Kui people in Phulbani, Odisha. During my stay in Shringarbhum between 1982–1987, I met women from villages deep inside the forest, who tattoo their entire faces. When asked the reason for this defacement, they said, 'to look ugly'. Not long ago, outsiders would come to their villages to pick women and abuse them. This was the 'only way to protect ourselves'.

In Phulbani, Odisha, several Kuttia Khonds, without my asking, wanted me to see on site the residues of a recent human sacrifice. This went on for several months. This was very awkward for me. Why did people want me to see these sites, I wondered. On careful listening, I discovered that the Kuttia Khonds have been frequently visited by a variety of researchers. Over time, the Khond people learnt all their questions and the expected answers. One most frequently asked question was: Is there any evidence of human sacrifice? In their perception, I too was a researcher, and this is why they thought I would like to see these sites.

My being non-judgemental created conditions for an open conversation about this practice. The Khonds denied knowledge of any cultural practice involving the ritual killing of human beings. The cultural phenomenon described by the people related to the natural death of people, the causes of which were different from the routine (ageing, disease, illness). For instance, I was told of men and women who would go into the forest for no specific task and not return. This was described as 'the spirits of the forest have taken human beings as an offering'.

Why did the Khonds not refute the incorrect representation by researchers of their 'ritual killing of human beings' and present the correct description of the phenomenon? What other course of action was available to the Koitor and other Adivasi women apart from defacing themselves?

As I see it, perpetuating the narrative of the 'ritual killing of human beings' is a form of suffocation that tribal people suffered in order to safeguard the cultural phenomenon of the 'natural death' of human beings in non-routine circumstances. Likewise, the tattooing of women's faces to look ugly is an expression of trauma resulting from social suffocation. Both are instances of defacement. In both instances there is pain that comes from denouncing and demeaning of the body, the language, and the culture of the people. In both instances there is a suffocation of the means of coping with this pain—they are denied the speech through which to express their resentment and protest. In the prevalent power structure, the people are not in a position to protest or express their disagreement. In the first instance, trauma is expressed through defacement by tattoos and in the second, by a deceptive collective social-cultural representation. In both cases, the language by which an individual and a community deal with pain and loss is damaged. In the first case, tattooing indicates the difficulty in narrating the experience, and in the second, the collective deception conceals the narrative.

In these examples, trauma is registered on both the ontological (tattooing the face) and the epistemological (the untruth of human sacrifice) aspects of the Adivasi being-in-the-world.

Under these conditions insurgency and agency became inalienable shadows of each other. Agency, defined in terms of the benefits of mainstreaming, has generated its shadow, 'insurgency as agency'. This mimesis between agency and its shadow today determines the frame for the construction of the self of tribal people. It has also divided the nation vertically into the 'Red Corridor' on the eastern side and the monochromatic developmental landscape on the western side.

Deprived of expressions in their own language, the people were left with no option other than to choose between the mainstream and insurgency. One set of tribal people integrated with the mainstream, partaking of all its benefits and its misgivings. Large majorities were marginalised on account of migration, forced displacement, infrastructure building for development, and poor school education. For a section of the marginalised tribal people, this was a reason to integrate with the political left militants—the Naxalites and their most recent incarnation, the Maoists. In their view, agency lies in insurgency and not in the benefits of the mainstream.

To have 'no options in one's own language' is social asphyxiation, for it removes people's sense of being-in-the-world from its expressions in their language; and this is no different from the denial of oxygen to the human body. This is the 'injustice of not being heard' (Stauffer 2015). For being in 'ethical loneliness' (ibid.) is akin to unethical confinement, comparable to the high-security prisons for criminals and/or concentration camps. It is an assault on the ontological and epistemological core of their existence.

Each of these denials has been an assault on their being-in-the-world. The trauma from these assaults is registered on the three critical elements of being-in-the-world—the conscious and the imaginary; the subconscious and the symbolic; and the unconscious and the real. Isolation suffocated the 'conscious' self; mimetic assimilation replaced the 'symbolic' collective; and the violence of integration destroyed the organic 'real' body.

This trauma begins with not communicating in their own language with their children. It continues with the adoption of a majority language, a deliberate interruption of not only the transmission of their language to the next generation, but also restricting the domains in which the language can be used. It develops into 'forgetting that one has forgotten one's own language'.

As regards linguistic extinction, it occurs when the minority community begins to transform the spoken language by giving it a script and a dictionary so that it may have a position in the mainstream. This process of standardisation is propelled by the fact that peoples' languages have no place in the mainstream, and for this reason, languages without scripts had no place in the education system (Kumar 2019, 56).

seven

The Topsoil of Modern Social Life

What is worthy of conservation? To respond to this question, I draw upon conversations with my friends Vasant Phutane and the Koitors.

Vasant Phutane lives on his farm in Rawala Village, Amravati, near Nagpur, Maharashtra. He practises 'no intervention cultivation' following Masanobu Fukuoka's one-straw revolution (Fukuoka 2010).

> Near a small village on the island of Shikoku in southern Japan, Masanobu Fukuoka has been developing a method of natural farming which could help to reverse the degenerative momentum of modern agriculture. Natural farming requires no machines, no chemicals, and very little weeding. Mr. Fukuoka does not plow the soil or use prepared compost. He does not hold water in his rice fields throughout the growing season as farmers have done for centuries in the Orient and around the world. The soil of his fields has been left unplowed for over twenty-five years, yet their yields compare favorably with those of the most productive Japanese farms. His method of farming requires less labor than any other. It creates no pollution and does not require the use of fossil fuels. (Fukuoka 2001 [1978], xxi)

When asked about his views on conservation, Phutane said, 'My effort is to add as much topsoil as I can in my lifetime.'

Topsoil is two inches to six inches thick. It is composed of a high concentration of organic matter and microorganisms, and it is here that the earth's activity occurs. It takes several hundred years to add one inch of topsoil. Over approximately 500 years, on account of the 'trickle-down development paradigm', 25 billion tons of topsoil is lost every year across the world; 7 tons of topsoil is lost with the production of every 1 ton of food grain. In India, 5,534 million tons of topsoil is lost every year. The rate of loss is 16.4 tons per hectare every year.[1]

Over the course of several conversations during my stay in the forest of Shringarbhum (north Bastar), Koitor men and women, both young and among the elders, said that for the safekeeping of forest landscapes, reverence for the lifecycle of regeneration, along with the fading in and fading out of seasons, is necessary. Within this frame of reference, they say that the safekeeping of social life will be impossible if we remember everything, or if we forget everything. The civilisational task is to know what is worthy of remembering and what is worthy of forgetting; what is worthy of keeping and what in worthy of letting go. Both these aspects of care-oriented conservation labour and its teleology have been discussed earlier.

There are three sets of themes for discussion here: the consumption factor underlying the loss of topsoil; against the backdrop of this factor, the contours of a heritage grounded in the reverence for life; and aspects of a conservation habitus.

This chapter discusses the significance of language, labor, and self for generating and conserving the topsoil of modern social life.

CONSUMING THE 'I'

A conversation between conservation environmentalists and conservation architects is necessary to determine the nature and scope of conservation labor. Today in India, the labour of conservation undertaken with respect to site-specific issues is primarily a management exercise directed by instrumental regimes of conventions, recommendations, and charters formulated by the international community on the one hand, and the provisions of the Constitution of India on the other. Under these regimes, there is a separation of the reserves of nature (the domain of the environmentalist) and cultural heritage (the domain of conservation architects).

Each has their respective field of work, and their domain-specific knowledge and practices. Both work on sites of intractable conflicts between the expanding international division of labour of an industrial-military complex driven by uncompromising accelerations of labour on the one hand, and natural landscapes as well as inspirational monuments on the other. The dynamics of intractability can be understood from the escalation of differences into conflicts, violence, war, and terrorism. These sites are multiplying, and in all of them there is either a threat to or a destruction of natural landscapes, historical monuments, as well as human habitations.

The loss of topsoil sums up the totality of this dynamics—it does not allow time for rest and recuperation at all levels of social life. Conservation regimes (law and policy) can do very little to provide time for rest and recuperation for the 'I' driven by the accelerations. This 'I' is sustained by an international division of instrumental labour driven by the industrial-military complex. The insatiable appetite of this 'I' continues to destroy landscape forests, water bodies, deserts, and mountains, and creates a mass of waste and global warming. Some aspects of the insatiable 'I' are described here.

The population of the world is, as of 2022, growing at a rate of around 0.84 per cent per year (down from 1.05 per cent in 2020, 1.08 per cent in 2019, 1.10 per cent in 2018, and 1.12 per cent in 2017). The current population increase is estimated at *67 million people per year*.[2] On 15 November 2022, the world's population surpassed *eight billion people*. Jared Diamond (2008, 23) says:

> .... The real burden lies in the consumption of the one billion people who live in developed countries, who consume and produce waste 32 times higher than in [the] developing world. If the entire developing world were to catch up, world consumption would increase elevenfold.... A real world problem is that each of the 300 million Americans consumes as much as 32 Kenyans. With ten times the population the United States consumes 320 times more resources than Kenya does.

The fact on the ground is that the developing world is catching up, and gradually and 'progressively' becoming like the developed world. The race for increasing GDPs (Gross Domestic Product) and per capita incomes is internalising the consumption of the developed world.

What is the 'I' that can consume thirty-two times more than, for example, a Kenyan? This consuming 'I' is an inert totality, and preoccupied with the labour of enjoyment. The labour of enjoyment makes up the substance of the inert 'I' with four attributes of 'inert totality' (discussed in Chapter One). To reiterate, these are:

> A totality is defined as a being which, while radically distinct from the sum of its parts, is present in its entirety, in one form or another, in each of these parts, and which relates to itself either through its relation to one or more of its parts or through its relation to the relations between all or some of them.
>
> If this reality is created (a painting or a symphony are examples ...), it can exist only in the imaginary (l'imaginaire), that is to say, as the correlative of an act of imagination.
>
> The ontological status to which it lays claim by its very definition is that of the in-itself, the inert. The synthetic unity produced its appearance of not an activity, but only the vestige of a past action.
>
> Through its being-in-exteriority, the inert in-itself gnaws away at this appearance of unity; the passive totality is, in fact, eroded infinite divisibility. (Sartre 2004, 45)

The inert 'I', correlative of an act of imagination, is created through a 'pursuit of a sense of enjoyment'; 'the moment of acquiring the object represents the end, not the beginning of enjoyment'. Its normative is—what I desire is what I need. This inert 'I' brings to a closure the difference between need and false need, and engages with the administration of desires. For instance, 'I am Samsung' says an advertisement, which shows a Bollywood film star holding a Samsung mobile phone! Its ontological status, grounded by 'I am, therefore I shop' and ' I shop, therefore I am', decommissions 'I am, therefore I think', or 'I think, therefore I am', or 'I work, therefore I am', or 'I am, therefore I work'.

With the acquisition of the object of enjoyment, the 'I' is constructed not by any productive activity. For this reason, the consumption of enjoyment is bound to be unwholesome, and thus dissatisfying. Such dissatisfaction is not a reason for the 'I' to abandon shopping for objects of enjoyment. On the contrary, the shopping continues to feed off every dissatisfaction that remains as a vestige of a similar past act of consumption. This goes on and on, and as it continues to feed off the dissatisfactions, the 'I' becomes unreflexively active. The infinite divisibility and fragmentation of the dissatisfied 'I' produces inertness. This is, in fact, consuming the 'I'.

The substance of the labour of enjoyment (the totality of the inert 'I') comes from the totality of the objects shopped. This totality is radically distinct from the sum of its parts (the objects) and is present in its entirety, in one form or another, in each of these parts (objects), and which (the inert 'I') relates to itself either through its relation to one or more of its parts (objects) or through its relation to the relations between all or some of them (objects). The 'I' for this reason acquires the attributes of inertness from the material objects of enjoyment. With these attributes, the 'inert I' is thus pushed towards vulnerability, its productive capabilities decommissioned. This takes away productive time and space from the life of an individual, and what remains is inert time and space, filled by inert objects.

All such shopped objects that are made from concrete abstract nature are an integral part of the belongings of a person. These belongings are in fact the materials that are useful for the construction of time, space, place, and identity. Such objects run into several hundreds for low consumers and many thousands for high consumers. As the enjoyment of these objects becomes the substance of the 'I', it is distanced from all aspects of concrete natural landscapes (the forest, rivers, mountains, etc.). Consequently, the world of shopped objects present in the external world is now present in the inner world of the 'I'. None of these objects can reproduce, and all of them are subject to the process of obsolescence. The goods that define the 'I' have a product life ranging from a few days to a few years. No product is designed to last a lifetime. It is inert in that it is unable to reproduce itself, and also because it has meaning only as given by the user, and none of its own. When the product becomes obsolete, it may be recycled; if not, it will find its way to the waste dumping grounds. This is called 'planned obsolescence'. Other than the organic products, the rest accumulates as non-recyclable waste. The range extends from plastic water bottles to nuclear waste and large sick industrial establishments. These, in mass quantities, convert natural landscapes into wastelands.

All this is done at such speed (also known as rates of innovation) that it leaves little time for recovery and recuperation; thus there is fatigue, a corresponding build-up of vulnerability, and a progressive decline in resilience. Consequently, human productive capabilities that constitute the 'I' are decommissioned and replaced with the productive capability of the technological. The inert 'I' blissfully engaged in a relentless pursuit of enjoyment is 'unmind-full' that the speed/rapidity of shopping in fact sustains the production of a growing mass of debris.

Each of the eight billion people in the world needs to acquire this 'I', which is the mandate of labour teleology under neoliberalism. This 'I' has made inroads into the everyday lives of diverse cultural communities in the vicinity of the architectural conservation sites as well as in the wider social context. It has marked its presence on the traditions of secular and religious structures, artefacts, myths, legends, manuscripts, rituals, customary practices, beliefs, and memories. As a result, these traditions also contribute to the debris on their part. The inert 'I' has radicalised the identity of these traditions by mutual exclusion. Not all aspects of the traditions of these communities are therefore conducive to conservation.

Is All of Tradition Worthy of Becoming Heritage?

Today, those who are persuaded by the worldview from the right of the political Centre hold that the mandate of conservation is to protect traditions of long duration from the onslaught of modernity. In this worldview, there is an inadequate and inappropriate uneasiness with those aspects of these traditions that are discriminatory. Those persuaded by the worldview from the liberal Centre hold that the best of both traditions and modernity can be conserved, and those persuaded by the worldview of the left of the political Centre hold that all discriminatory and retrogressive elements of traditions are to be abandoned. In contemporary times, the differences between these positions have often rapidly escalated into conflicts, followed by violence.

None of these are concerned with either the inert I or with the loss of topsoil. The mandate for conservation in this situation cannot be determined by aligning with any of these positions. It will emerge in the course of constructing a 'social field' on the principle of reverence for life, over and above these positions. For this, it is necessary to recognise the distinction between heritage and tradition. In everyday usage, these words are interchangeable. A closer look shows a subtle difference.

The difference between '*parampara*' and '*virasat*' corresponds to the difference between 'tradition' and 'heritage'. Parampara (traditions) are the vestiges of past actions. These form a body of rules for modes of thinking, for codes of conduct, and for the classification of material artefacts for a group of people who share at least one or more of the following social attributes: language, religion, culture, class, status, and power. It tends towards exclusiveness.

Virasat (heritage) is a clear field accessible to a diversity of people, across differences in language, religion, class, status, and power. The rules that define it tend towards inclusiveness. Every tradition can contribute to the making of heritage. This happens when people of one tradition engage reciprocally with people from other traditions.

Corresponding to parampara and virasat, there are different notions of the 'social'. Very briefly, the social is the field determined by the relation between the individual and the collective. We know from experience that what is good for the individual is not always good for the collective, and what is good for the collective is not always good for the individual. Remembering and forgetting have an important role here.

Parampara is founded on memory. It is uncomfortable with forgetting. The good for the individual is in complete compliance with that of the collective. Here, the possibility of negotiation (between the individual and the collective) is restricted: customary/ legal regimes insulate the residues of ancestors from interacting with the contemporary wider social context. A significant attribute of these regimes is the habit of 'not letting go', and transferring practices, experience, occurrences, any materials and/or ideas that are part of an individual as well as a collective biography to the realm of forgetting. These regimes are based on and perpetuate the separation of non-human nature and culture. Historical experience over 200 years has demonstrated that this leads to disaster, generates violence, and damages life processes irrecoverably. Here, injustices (addressed and/or unaddressed) cannot be sorted and consigned to the realm of forgetting; over generations, this wears out and exhausts human social structures, culture, and the spirit, which precipitates an 'irreverence for life'.

These regimes are designed to protect, maintain, and safeguard the physical structures. For instance, the 1954 Hague Convention for the Protection of Cultural Property in the Event of Armed Conflict makes provision for the protection of monuments and sites. These sites are distributed over two distinct categories of nature and culture. There are different programmes for each. For instance, the conservation of forests and conservation of tribal culture are two different programmes located in distinct places—the forest and outside the forest. This is insensitive to their mutual embeddedness. This separation is the basis of the contemporary political and economic systems designed to overpower nature, and these sites are, for these reasons, assimilated into the political economies of unmitigated waste reproduction. Procedures of protection deprive a substantial number of people of their livelihoods, and turn these sites into exotic parts of consumerism. The separation of nature and culture is a violation of the integrity of the exchanges between them.

Virasat begins to take shape when the interplay between memory and forgetting begins to open up space and time for negotiation, and building up reciprocal relations between the individual and the collective. There is anxiety to ensure that what is good for the individual does not come into conflict with the collective, and vice-versa. This negotiability forms the foundation of fair-mindedness. Fair-mindedness measures potentiality through the parameters of worthiness, adequacy, and appropriateness of the limits of the relations between the individual and the collective; how far can it be extended to explore the potentiality of the 'yet to come'? Fair-mindedness is a particular instance of 'potentiality'. Its meaning and significance emerge when the limits are extended from being in the here and now to being in the yet to come, the yet to be realised.

Potentiality has 'outstanding value', inclusive of nature and culture. The outstanding value of heritage sites emerges from the togetherness of nature and culture. There are four attributes of outstanding value: time; foundational position; steadfastness; and inclusive transcendental presence.

The heritage of the togetherness of nature and culture unfolds over a long duration of time rhythms, ranging from a few hundred years to a few thousand years. This brings a sense of dignity, of steadfastness, and freshness, shaped by having withstood the wear and tear of time. This illuminates the value and meaningfulness of every other thing in the world. In its absence, the lives of millions are likely to be affected adversely. In this worldview, they are in a foundational position. The particular geography and contexts in which they are situated highlight their creative energies. These belong to no one, but all can belong here, everyone can draw from it the energy to rejuvenate. All of this makes their presence inclusive and transcendental. This holds potentiality. The togetherness of these attributes forms the potentiality of 'life processes', understood as the limits 'yet to come', which are 'not yet framed'.

Conservation is a political intervention that contributes to the making of virasat. It allows for the negotiation between the individual and the collective. Protection becomes conservation when it is concerned with the worthiness of the outstanding value—how mindful it is of the potential of the reciprocal relation between human beings and nature. Meaningful conservation is determined by practices that can generate livelihoods by upholding the worthiness of the outstanding value of life as such.

Conservation practices thus negotiate the place for the outstanding value of heritage in a world of wasteful consumption, create for it an appropriate position in people's worldview, and prepare the ground for making conservation a habit which goes beyond not wasting, not generating waste, recycling, the economic use of resources, and cost-effectiveness. Conservation habits based on a 'reverence for life' uphold the reciprocity between the world of nature and the world of culture in our social lives across the spectrum, extending from our daily activities to collective public works. Today, efforts to make conservation a totally commercial activity have destroyed its core, because the inability to generate sufficient funds makes it impossible to undertake any such attempts.

Five Aspects of Topsoil

Conservation habitus in everyday life is the edifice for our well-being.

Our 'habitus' constitutes us as 'beings with habits'—attitudes, emotions, practices, rituals, customs, thinking habits, material culture, ways of earning a livelihood, social relations, and so on. This habitus defines the work of a conservationist in the likeness of organic gardening, that is, to create conditions for the mutuality between both human and non-human, to unfold in the time and space of history.

A conservation habitus comes into being gradually, directing the teleology of labor with care. This teleology is enriched with the interplay between memory and forgetting. The conservation habitus, in my view, has five aspects: shelter, parsimony, resilience, elasticity, and plurality. They are aspects of a habit as well as of a structure and system. A shelter both protects and looks after. It regulates the relation between the inside and the outside of a structure and system, and has a physical as well as a social and cultural aspect. As a habit, to give shelter is to generate the warmth necessary for recovery. Our memories (in the form of ideas, events, material culture, and social processes) can generate warmth as much as an ability to forget. The past that remains with us can be both a curse and a blessing. Memories can cause illness as much as they can heal.

There are so many situations wherein good theory and poetry can combine! Imagine our condition if the historical landscape was either cluttered with material remains or if there was nothing that remained from the past. Equally, imagine our condition if, in the search for everlasting life and unbroken continuity, we were to either forget all that went into making us what we are today or we were unable to forget anything at all. To remember or to forget can haunt as much as it can rejuvenate. Under such conditions, there is no shelter and civil life is not possible.

Parsimony prevents the dissipation of materials, efforts, energy, and symbolic capital. It is an aspect of work culture that needs to be cultivated in order to deal with and restrain our wasteful habits. What is alarming is the speed of development; the rate at which injuries are inflicted is faster than the rate at which people can recover (with all the support systems). Such wounds and scars do not heal for several generations. As our vulnerability to crisis increases, our cultural reserves are depleted and capacities for recuperation diminish. Instead of generating a creative and constructive social force, contradictions and conflicts destroy the self, society, and human and non-human nature.

Resilience is an attribute of the materials used for conservation and of a system that is constructed on sound internal principles. This provides stability and over time, adds to grandeur. What is significant is the rapidity with which differences degenerate into conflict, conflict into violence, and how war and terrorism mirror each other. Human beings are reduced to thinking of themselves as wronged and ill-treated. Annihilation and absolute negation determine the relation between individuals, groups, and nations, and between humans and nature. For instance, victims of social conflict and violence pay back their oppressors in the same coin. In the process, they become like their oppressors and reproduce the social and material conditions that were responsible for their oppression in the first place. This vicious cycle of violence continually reproduces itself. As a consequence, over time, human beings become vulnerable.

Where crises, breakdowns, and disasters multiply, human beings begin thinking of themselves as victims and not as the makers of civilisations and history. The pursuit of freedom by 'one' can then result in terror for the other; plurality is favourable for recovery, conversation, and dialogue. This is because plurality is being respectful to differences and harnesses opposing forces generated from differences.

This habitus thus nourishes and is in turn nourished by a stable multilingualism.

> Stable multilingualism in India may perhaps be interpreted as a general form of diglossia. That is domain-specific use of different languages or different styles or the same language within a community (Ferguson 1959).... The respective domains of family, neighborhood, education, work and play cannot be readily arranged hierarchically. To ask which of them is more important or more prestigious ... is to impose a wholly false set of alternatives.... In a stable bilingual situation people develop ways of speaking in which they can maintain their own language and still communicate with speakers of other languages. The use of different languages is not congruent, equal or parallel in all spheres of activity. On the contrary, the pattern of use of languages in a bilingual community[is] largely complementary [Pandit 1976]. (Uberoi and Tyabji 2019, 97)
>
> The various languages at the speaker's command complement one another, and no single language is expected to fulfill all the functions of everyday communications. (ibid., 101)

Further, Uberoi points out, 'Custom ... represents the will of the people and it also rules their conduct' and, 'custom, not natural instinct or universal reason, was the ruling force in civil society' (ibid., 126).

'To Belong' is Faith in the Nature of Things

The universe of the forest tree evokes reverence—such is its magnificence. Its shade and shadow evoke faith, love, compassion, and commitment. Trees contour a sheltering landscape, and for this, they are worthy of reverence and veneration.

People who live, or attempt to live, alongside landscape rhythms recognise the presence of sentient beings in all its elements. The seamless in every element—stones, dust, hills, water, plants, animals, and everything else there is—is an expression of life. From each, everything acquires its 'presence'. Each therefore belongs to the every, partakes of the every, and absorbs the every. Its being alive makes it a living space.

There is no 'other'. This differentiates it from a landmass. The nature-abiding people in reverence propitiate trees, stones, hills, waterholes, rivers, earth, fire, wind, and sky. In this, the abiding tenet is: 'to belong is in the nature of things as an expression of faith'. This is an attunement of each in the safekeeping of everything, as much as it is of everything in the safekeeping of each element.

An instance of such a landscape is the 'forestscape' of Shringarbhum, in north Bastar, Chhattisgarh. Its architectural contours run alongside the life processes of the universe of the forest. The work of Talurmuttee—mother earth—decorates Shringarbhum. At her altar, made at the base of a sal tree (*Shorea robusta*) in the forest, Koitors annually come together to celebrate the beginning and the completion of the cultivation cycle. Collectively, they make their meals, eat, and leave behind leaf plates for her to see and know their attunement to her work. To belong here is their faith; with this, they acquire a presence in the forest.

There is faith in the nature of the tree—its propensity to reach out into the sky, offer fruits, flowers, as well as shade and shelter, and be firmly grounded. Its grounded-ness brings to it all life forms, to rest and nest in its shade. The 'becoming and being' of people is cast in the image of a tree. Such belonging is an expression of being tuned-in. On account of their attunement to living alongside the life rhythms and rhymes of this universe, Koitors' belongings comprise as much as they can bring along the forest paths, to the trees, plants, animals, birds, the stones, and the hills. These offerings (to the forest paths, the trees, plants, animals, birds, the stones, the hills) attune Koitor lives to this universe. Such attunement is a mode of belonging.

Given the nature of things, attunement brings with it the propensity to lose and then retrieve one's path. The seamlessness of forest landscapes shelters—disguises, conceals, covers up, masks, obscures—everything from everything else, only for each to rest and to nest with everything. It is like having a sense of one's own presence while at the same time not forgoing the sense of togetherness with everything else.

In the village, Talurmuttee resides in the ghotul. This is a space where, under her shelter, boys and girls make a hut and grow up to become responsible, mature members of society. As soon as the child, boy and girl, begins to understand household work, they are sent to the ghotul. Here, they are given a ghotul name, which defines their membership to an age group and inaugurates their socialisation into the ways of living in society. A ghotul member learns all aspects of social life. The ghotul comes alive after sunset, when households prepare to rest and nest. Boys and girls light a fire and gather to dance, sing, and exchange conversations.

In both places—the forest and the ghotul—the self-activity of the earth is celebrated. Its seamlessness shelters all life forms. This is a condition for the nature of things to manifest as an expression of faith. This seamlessness is attuned to the rhythm of life processes. The labor of childbirth is attuned to mother earth. When labor pains begin, women move across the earth, from one spot to another, until they reach a part where the child comes into the universe of the forest. Conversely, where you do not belong, birthing will not happen. To belong is to be attuned to.

Like the labor of childbirth, all forms of labor are modes of attunement. Labor attunes the imaginations to the width and depth of the universe of the forest.

Endnotes

1. Industrial farming practices such as tilling and the use of agrochemicals, as well as deforestation to produce farmland have dramatically increased the rate of soil erosion. Around the world, topsoil is vanishing much faster than it forms. According to David Montgomery, a geologist at the University of Washington, it is clear that we are losing more and more topsoil every day: 'The estimate is that we are now losing about 1 percent of our topsoil every year to erosion, most of this caused by agriculture.' The United States is losing soil at a rate ten times faster than the soil replenishment rate, while China and India are losing soil thirty to forty times faster. With soil erosion rates so much higher than the replenishment rate, it is no wonder that the world is quickly running out of fertile topsoil (Verso 2015).

2. See https://www.worldometers.info/world-population/ (accessed June 2023).

Appendix I

The Provisions of the Panchayats (Extension to the Scheduled Areas) Act, 1996 No. 40 of 1996 (24 December 1996)

An Act to provide for the extension of the provisions of Part IX of the Constitution relating to the Panchayats to the Scheduled Areas.

Be it enacted by Parliament in the Forty-seventh Year of the Republic of India as follows:

Short title

1. This Act may be called the Provisions of the Panchayats (Extension to the Scheduled Areas) Act, 1996

Definition

2. In this Act, unless the context otherwise requires, 'Scheduled Areas' means the Scheduled Areas as referred to in Clause (1) of Article 244 of the Constitution.

Extension of Part IX of the Constitution

3. The provision of Part IX of the Constitution relating to Panchayats are hereby extended to the Scheduled Areas subject to such exceptions and modifications as are provided in section 4.

Exceptions and modifications to Part IX of the Constitution

4. Notwithstanding anything contained under Part IX of the Constitution, the Legislature of a State shall not make any law under that Part which is inconsistent with any of the following features, namely:
   (a) A State legislation on the Panchayats that may be made shall be in consonance with the customary law, social and religious practices and traditional management practices of community resources;
   (b) A village shall ordinarily consist of a habitation or a group of habitations or a hamlet or a group of hamlets comprising a community and managing its affairs in accordance with traditions and customs;
   (c) Every village shall have a Gram Sabha consisting of persons whose names are included in the electoral rolls for the Panchayat at the village level;
   (d) Every Gram Sabha shall be competent to safeguard and preserve the traditions and customs of the people, their cultural identity, community resources and the customary mode of dispute resolution;
   (e) Every Gram Sabha shall—
      i. approve of the plans, programmes and projects for social and economic development before such plans, programmes and projects are taken up for implementation by the Panchayat at the village level;
      ii. be responsible for the identification or selection of persons as beneficiaries under the poverty alleviation and other programmes;
   (f) Every Panchayat at the village level shall be required to obtain from the Gram Sabha a certification of utilisation of funds by that Panchayat for the plans, programmes and projects referred to in clause (e);
   (g) The reservation of seats in the Scheduled Areas at every Panchayat shall be in proportion to the population of the communities in that Panchayat for whom reservation is sought to be given under Part IX of the Constitution;

Provided that the reservation for the Scheduled Tribes shall not be less than one-half of the total number of seats;

Provided further that all seats of Chairpersons of Panchayats at all levels shall be reserved for the Scheduled Tribes;

(h) The State Government may nominate persons belonging to such Scheduled Tribes as have no representation in the Panchayat at the intermediate level or the Panchayat at the district level:

Provided that such nomination shall not exceed one-tenth of the total members to be elected in that Panchayat;

(i) The Gram Sabha or the Panchayats at the appropriate level shall be consulted before making the acquisition of land in the Scheduled Areas for development projects and before re-settling or rehabilitating persons affected by such projects in the Scheduled Areas; the actual planning and implementation of the projects in the Scheduled Areas shall be coordinated at the State level;

(j) Planning and management of minor water bodies in the Scheduled Areas shall be entrusted to Panchayats at the appropriate level;

(k) The recommendations of the Gram Sabha or the Panchayats at the appropriate level shall be made mandatory prior to grant of prospecting licence or mining lease for minor minerals in the Scheduled Areas;

(l) The prior recommendation of the Gram Sabha or the Panchayats at the appropriate level shall be made mandatory for grant of concession for the exploitation of minor minerals by auction;

(m) While endowing Panchayats in the Scheduled Areas with such powers and authority as may be necessary to enable them to function as institutions of self-government, a State Legislature shall ensure that the Panchayats at the appropriate level and the Gram Sabha are endowed specifically with—

(i) The power to enforce prohibition or to regulate or restrict the sale and consumption of any intoxicant;
(ii) The ownership of minor forest produce;
(iii) The power to prevent alienation of land in the Scheduled Areas and to take appropriate action to restore any unlawfully alienated land of a Scheduled Tribe;
(iv) The power to manage village markets by whatever name called;
(v) The power to exercise control over money lending to the Scheduled Tribes;
(vi) The power to exercise control over institutions and functionaries in all social sectors;
(vii) The power to control over [*sic*] local plans and resources for such plans including tribal sub-plans;

(n) The State Legislations that may endow Panchayats with powers and authority as may be necessary to enable them to function as institutions of self-government shall contain safeguards to ensure that Panchayats at the higher level do not assume the powers and authority of any Panchayat at the lower level or of the Gram Sabha;

(o) The State Legislature shall endeavour to follow the pattern of the Sixth Schedule to the Constitution while designing the administrative arrangements in the Panchayats at district levels in the Scheduled Areas.

Continuance of existing laws on panchayats:

5. Notwithstanding anything in Part IX of the Constitution with exceptions and modifications made by this Act, any provision of any law relating to Panchayats in force in the Scheduled Areas, immediately before the date on which this Act receives the assent of the President, which is inconsistent with the provisions of Part IX with such exceptions and modifications shall continue to be in force until amended or repealed by a competent Legislature or other competent authority or until the expiration of one year from the date on which this Act receives the assent of the President;

Provided that all the Panchayats existing immediately before such date shall continue till the expiration of their duration unless sooner dissolved by a resolution passed to that effect by the Legislative Assembly of that State or, in the case of a State having Legislative Council, by each House of the Legislature of that State.

K. L. MOHANPURIA,
Secy. to the Govt. of India

Appendix II

Forest Rights Act, 2006: Act, Rules and Guidelines

Short title and commencement

1. (1) This Act may be called the Scheduled Tribes and Other Traditional Forest Dwellers (Recognition of Forest Rights) Act, 2006.
   (2) It extends to the whole of India except the State of Jammu and Kashmir.
   (3) It shall come into force on such date as the Central Government may, by notification in the Official Gazette, appoint.

Definitions

2. In this Act, unless the context otherwise requires,
   (a) 'community forest resource' means customary common forest land within the traditional or customary boundaries of the village or seasonal use of landscape in the case of pastoral communities, including reserved forests, protected forests and protected areas such as Sanctuaries and National Parks to which the community had traditional access;
   (b) 'critical wildlife habitat' means such areas of National Parks and Sanctuaries where it has been specifically and clearly established, case by case, on the basis of scientific and objective criteria, that such areas are required to be kept as inviolate for the purposes of wildlife conservation as may be determined and notified by the Central Government in the Ministry of

Environment and Forests after open process of consultation by an Expert Committee, which includes experts from the locality appointed by that Government wherein a representative of the Ministry of Tribal Affairs shall also be included, in determining such areas according to the procedural requirements arising from sub-sections (1) and (2) of section 4;

(c) 'forest dwelling Scheduled Tribes' means the members or community of the Scheduled Tribes who primarily reside in and who depend on the forests or forest lands for *bona fide* livelihood needs and includes the Scheduled Tribe pastoralist communities;

(d) 'forest land' means land of any description falling within any forest area and includes unclassified forests, un-demarcated forests, existing or deemed forests, protected forests, reserved forests, Sanctuaries and National Parks;

(e) 'forest rights' means the forest rights referred to in section 3;

(f) 'forest villages' means the settlements which have been established inside the forests by the forest department of any State Government for forestry operations or which were converted into forest villages through the forest reservation process and includes forest settlement villages, fixed demand holdings, all types of *taungya* settlements, by whatever name called, for such villages and includes lands for cultivation and other uses permitted by the Government;

(g) 'Gram Sabha' means a village assembly which shall consist of all adult members of a village and in case of States having no Panchayats, Padas, Tolas and other traditional village institutions and elected village committees, with full and unrestricted participation of women;

(h) 'habitat' includes the area comprising the customary habitat and such other habitats in reserved forests and protected forests of primitive tribal groups and pre-agricultural communities and other forest dwelling Scheduled Tribes;

(i) 'minor forest produce' includes all non-timber forest produce of plant origin including bamboo, brush wood, stumps, cane, tussar, cocoons, honey, wax, lac, tendu or kendu leaves, medicinal plants and herbs, roots, tubers and the like;

(j) 'nodal agency' means the nodal agency specified in section 11;

(k) 'notification' means a notification published in the Official Gazette;

(l) 'prescribed' means prescribed by rules made under this Act;

(m) 'Scheduled Areas' means the Scheduled Areas referred to in clause (l) of Article 244 of the Constitution;

(n) 'sustainable use' shall have the same meaning as assigned to it in clause (o) of Section 2 of the Biological Diversity Act, 2002;

(o) 'other traditional forest dweller' means any member or community who has for at least three generations prior to the 13th day of December, 2005 primarily resided in and who depend on the forest or forests land for *bona fide* livelihood needs.

Explanation: For the purpose of this clause, 'generation' means a period comprising of twenty-five years.

(p) 'village' means:–

(i) a village referred to in clause (b) of Section 4 of the Provisions of the Panchayats (Extension to the Scheduled Areas) Act, 1996; or

(ii) any area referred to as a village in any State law relating to Panchayats other than the Scheduled Areas; or

(iii) forest villages, old habitation or settlements and unsurveyed villages, whether notified as village or not; or

(iv) in the case of States where there are no Panchayats, the traditional village, by whatever name called;

(q) 'wild animal' means any species of animal specified in Schedules I to IV of the Wild Life (Protection) Act, 1972 and found wild in nature.

Chapter II: Forest Rights

3. (1) For the purposes of this Act, the following rights, which secure individual or community tenure or both, shall be the

forest rights of forest dwelling Scheduled Tribes and other traditional forest dwellers on all forest lands, namely:

(a) right to hold and live in the forest land under the individual or common occupation for habitation or for self-cultivation for livelihood by a member or members of a forest dwelling Scheduled Tribe or other traditional forest dwellers;
(b) community rights such as *nistar*, by whatever name called, including those used in erstwhile Princely States, Zamindari or such intermediary regimes;
(c) right of ownership, access to collect, use, and dispose of minor forest produce which has been traditionally collected within or outside village boundaries;
(d) other community rights of uses or entitlements such as fish and other products of water bodies, grazing (both settled or transhumant) and traditional seasonal resource access of nomadic or pastoralist communities;
(e) rights including community tenures of habitat and habitation for primitive tribal groups and pre-agricultural communities;
(f) rights in or over disputed lands under any nomenclature in any State where claims are disputed;
(g) rights for conversion of *Pattas* or leases or grants issued by any local authority or any State Government on forest lands to titles;
(h) rights of settlement and conversion of all forest villages, old habitation, unsurveyed villages and other villages in forests, whether recorded, notified or not into revenue villages;
(i) rights to protect, regenerate or conserve or manage any community forest resource which they have been traditionally protecting and conserving for sustainable use;
(j) rights which are recognised under any State law or laws of any Autonomous District Council or Autonomous Regional Council or which are accepted as rights of tribal [*sic*] under any traditional or customary law of the concerned tribes of any State;

(k) right of access to biodiversity and community right to intellectual property and traditional knowledge related to biodiversity and cultural diversity;

(l) any other traditional right customarily enjoyed by the forest dwelling Scheduled Tribes or other traditional forest dwellers, as the case may be, which are not mentioned in clauses (a) to (k) but excluding the traditional right of hunting or trapping or extracting a part of the body of any species of wild animal;

(m) right to *in situ* rehabilitation including alternative land in cases where the Scheduled Tribes or other traditional forest dwellers have been illegally evicted or displaced from forest land of any description without receiving their legal entitlement to rehabilitation prior to the 13th day of December, 2005.

(2) Notwithstanding anything contained in the Forest (Conservation) Act, 1980, the Central Government shall provide for diversion of forest land for the following facilities managed by the Government which involve felling of trees not exceeding seventy-five trees per hectare, namely:-

(a) schools;
(b) dispensary or hospital;
(c) anganwadis;
(d) fair price shops;
(e) electric and telecommunication lines;
(f) tanks and other minor water bodies;
(g) drinking water supply and water pipelines;
(h) water or rain water harvesting structures;
(i) minor irrigation canals;
(j) non-conventional source of energy;
(k) skill up-gradation or vocational training centers;
(l) roads; and
(m) community centers:

Provided that such diversion of forest land shall be allowed only if—

(i) the forest land to be diverted for the purposes mentioned in this subsection is less than one hectare in each case; and

(ii) the clearance of such developmental projects shall be subject to the condition that the same is recommended by the Gram Sabha.

Chapter III: Recognition, Restoration and Vesting of Forest Rights and Related Matters

4. (1) Notwithstanding anything contained in any other law for the time being in force, and subject to the provisions of this Act, the Central Government hereby recognises and vests forest rights in—
   (a) the forest dwelling Scheduled Tribes in States or areas in States where they are declared as Scheduled Tribes in respect of all forest rights mentioned in section 3;
   (b) the other traditional forest dwellers in respect of all forest rights mentioned in section 3.

(2) The forest rights recognised under this Act in critical wildlife habitats of National Parks and Sanctuaries may subsequently be modified or resettled, provided that no forest rights holders shall be resettled or have their rights in any manner affected for the purposes of creating inviolate areas for wildlife conservation except in case all the following conditions are satisfied, namely:
   (a) the process of recognition and vesting of rights as specified in section 6 is complete in all the areas under consideration;
   (b) it has been established by the concerned agencies of the State Government, in exercise of their powers under the Wild Life (Protection) Act, 1972 that the activities or impact of the presence of holders of rights upon wild animals is sufficient to cause irreversible damage and threaten the existence of said species and their habitat;
   (c) the State Government has concluded that other reasonable options, such as, co-existence are not available;

(d) a resettlement or alternatives package has been prepared and communicated that provides a secure livelihood for the affected individuals and communities and fulfils the requirements of such affected individuals and communities given in the relevant laws and the policy of the Central Government;

(e) the free informed consent of the Gram Sabhas in the areas concerned to the proposed resettlement and to the package has been obtained in writing;

(f) no resettlement shall take place until facilities and land allocation at the resettlement location are complete as per the promised package;

Provided that the critical wildlife habitats from which rights holders are thus relocated for purposes of wildlife conservation shall not be subsequently diverted by the State Government or the Central Government or any other entity for other uses.

(3) The recognition and vesting of forest rights under this Act to the forest dwelling Scheduled Tribes and to other traditional forest dwellers in relation to any State or Union Territory in respect of forest land and their habitat shall be subject to the condition that such Scheduled Tribes or tribal communities or other traditional forest dwellers had occupied forest land before the 13th day of December, 2005.

(4) A right conferred by sub-section (1) shall be heritable but not alienable or transferable and shall be registered jointly in the name of both the spouses in case of married persons and in the name of the single head in the case of a household headed by a single person and in the absence of a direct heir, the heritable right shall pass on to the next-of-kin.

(5) Save as otherwise provided, no member of a forest dwelling Scheduled Tribe or other traditional forest dweller shall be evicted or removed from forest land under his occupation till the recognition and verification procedure is complete.

(6) Where the forest rights recognised and vested by sub- section (1) are in respect of land mentioned in clause (a) of sub-section (1) of section 3 such land shall be under the occupation of an individual or family or community on the date of

commencement of this Act and shall be restricted to the area under actual occupation and shall in no case exceed an area of four hectares.

(7) The forest rights shall be conferred free of all encumbrances and procedural requirements, including clearance under the Forest (Conservation) Act, 1980, requirement of paying the 'net present value' and 'compensatory afforestation' for diversion of forest land, except those specified in this Act.

(8) The forest rights recognised and vested under this Act shall include the right of land to forest dwelling Scheduled Tribes and other traditional forest dwellers who can establish that they were displaced from their dwelling and cultivation without land compensation due to State development interventions, and where the land has not been used for the purpose for which it was acquired within five years of the said acquisition.

4. The holders of any forest right, Gram Sabha and village level institutions in areas where there are holders of any forest right under this Act are empowered to—

(a) protect the wild life, forest and biodiversity;

(b) ensure that adjoining catchments area, water sources and other ecological sensitive areas are adequately protected;

(c) ensure that the habitat of forest dwelling Scheduled Tribes and other traditional forest dwellers is preserved from any form of destructive practices affecting their cultural and natural heritage;

(d) ensure that the decisions taken in the Gram Sabha to regulate access to community forest resources and stop any activity which adversely affects the wild animals, forest and the biodiversity are complied with.

Chapter IV: Authorities and Procedure for Vesting of Forest Rights

6. (1) The Gram Sabha shall be the authority to initiate the process for determining the nature and extent of individual or

community forest rights or both that may be given to the forest dwelling Scheduled Tribes and other traditional forest dwellers within the local limits of its jurisdiction under this Act by receiving claims, consolidating and verifying them and preparing a map delineating the area of each recommended claim in such manner as may be prescribed for exercise of such rights and the Gram Sabha shall, then, pass a resolution to that effect and thereafter forward a copy of the same to the Sub-Divisional Level Committee.

(2) Any person aggrieved by the resolution of the Gram Sabha may prefer a petition to the Sub-Divisional Level Committee constituted under sub-section (3) and the Sub-Divisional Level Committee shall consider and dispose of such petition.

Provided that every such petition shall be preferred within sixty days from the date of passing of the resolution by the Gram Sabha:

Provided further that no such petition shall be disposed of against the aggrieved person, unless he has been given a reasonable opportunity to present his case.

(3) The State Government shall constitute a Sub-Divisional Level Committee to examine the resolution passed by the Gram Sabha and prepare the record of forest rights and forward it through the Sub-Divisional Officer to the District Level Committee for a final decision.

(4) Any person aggrieved by the decision of the Sub-Divisional Level Committee may prefer a petition to the District Level Committee within sixty days from the date of decision of the Sub-Divisional Level Committee and the District Level Committee shall consider and dispose of such petition:

Provided that no petition shall be preferred directly before the District Level Committee against the resolution of the Gram Sabha unless the same has been preferred before and considered by the Sub-Divisional level Committee:

Provided further that no such petition shall be disposed of against the aggrieved person, unless he has been given a reasonable opportunity to present his case.

(5) The State Government shall constitute a District Level Committee to consider and finally approve the record of forest rights prepared by the Sub-Divisional Level Committee.

(6) The decision of the District Level Committee on the record of forest rights shall be final and binding.

(7) The State Government shall constitute a State Level Monitoring Committee to monitor the process of recognition and vesting of forest rights and to submit to the nodal agency such returns and reports as may be called for by that agency.

(8) The Sub-Divisional Level Committee, the District Level Committee and the State Level Monitoring Committee shall consist of officers of the department of Revenue, Forest and Tribal Affairs of the State Government and three members of the Panchayati Raj Institutions at the appropriate level, appointed by the respective Panchayati Raj Institutions, of whom two shall be the Scheduled Tribe members and at least one shall be a woman, as may be prescribed.

(9) The composition and functions of the Sub-Divisional Level Committee, the District Level Committee and the State Level Monitoring Committee and the procedure to be followed by them in the discharge of their functions shall be such as may be prescribed.

Chapter V: Offences and Penalties

7. Where any authority or Committee or officer or member of such authority or Committee contravenes any provision of this Act or any rule made thereunder concerning recognition of forest rights, it, or they, shall be deemed to be guilty of an offence under this Act and shall be liable to be proceeded against and punished with fine which may extend to one thousand rupees:

8. No court shall take cognizance of any offence under section 7 unless any forest dwelling Scheduled Tribe in case of a dispute relating to a resolution of a Gram Sabha or the Gram Sabha

through a resolution against any higher authority gives a notice of not less than sixty days to the State Level Monitoring Committee and the State Level Monitoring Committee has not proceeded against such authority.

Chapter VI: Miscellaneous

9. Every member of the authorities referred to in Chapter IV and every other officer exercising any of the powers conferred by or under this Act shall be deemed to be a public servant within the meaning of section 21 of the Indian Penal Code.
10. (1) No suit, prosecution or other legal proceeding shall lie against any officer or other employee of the Central Government or the State Government for anything which is in good faith done or intended to be done by or under this Act.
    (2) No suit or other legal proceeding shall lie against the Central Government or the State Government or any of its officers or other employees for any damage caused or likely to be caused by anything which is in good faith done or intended to be done under this Act.
    (3) No suit or other legal proceeding shall lie against any authority as referred to in Chapter IV including its Chairperson, members, member-secretary, officers and other employees for anything which is in good faith done or intended to be done under this Act.
11. The Ministry of the Central Government dealing with Tribal Affairs or any officer or authority authorised by the Central Government in this behalf shall be the nodal agency for the implementation of the provisions of this Act.
12. In the performance of its duties and exercise of its powers by or under this Act, every authority referred to in Chapter IV shall be subject to such general or special directions, as the Central Government may, from time to time, give in writing.
13. Save as otherwise provided in this Act and the Provisions of the Panchayats (Extension to the Scheduled Areas) Act, 1996, the

provisions of this Act shall be in addition to and not in derogation of the provisions of any other law for the time being in force.

14. (1) The Central Government may; by notification, and subject to the condition of previous publication, make rules for carrying out the provisions of this Act.

(2) In particular, and without prejudice to the generality of the foregoing powers, such rules may provide for all any of the following matters, namely:

(a) procedural details for implementation of the procedure specified in section 6;

(b) the procedure for receiving claims, consolidating and verifying them and preparing a map delineating the area of each recommended claim for exercise of forest rights under sub-section (1) of section 6 and the manner of preferring a petition to the Sub-Divisional Committee under sub-section (2) of that section;

(c) the level of officers of the departments of Revenue, Forest and Tribal Affairs of the State Government to be appointed as members of the Sub-Divisional Level Committee, the District Level Committee and the State Level Monitoring Committee under sub- section (8) of section 6;

(d) the composition and functions of the Sub-Divisional Level Committee, the District Level Committee and the State Level Monitoring Committee and the procedure to be followed by them in the discharge of their functions under sub-section (9) of section 6;

(e) any other matter which is required to be, or may be, prescribed.

(3) Every rule made by the Central Government under this Act shall be laid, as soon as may be after it is made, before each House of Parliament, while it is in session, for a total period of thirty days which may be comprised in one session or in two or more successive sessions, and if, before the expiry of the session immediately following the session or the successive sessions aforesaid, both Houses agree in making any modification in the rule or both Houses agree that the

rule should not be made, the rule shall thereafter have effect only in such modified form or be of no effect, as the case may be; so however, that any such modification or annulment shall be without prejudice to the validity of anything previously done under that rule.

K. N. CHATURVEDI,
Secy. to the Govt. of India.

Bibliography

Abram, David. 1997. *The Spell of the Sensuous*. New York: Vintage Books.

Agamben, Giorgio. 1999. *Potentialities: Collected Essays in Philosophy*, Daniel Heller-Roazen (ed. and trans.). Stanford: Stanford University Press.

Arya, Shachi. 1998. *Tribal Activism: Voices of Protest*. Jaipur and New Delhi: Rawat Publications.

Bachram, Heidi. 2004. 'Climate Fraud and Carbon Colonialism: The New Trade in Greenhouse Gases'. *Capitalism Nature and Socialism* 15 (4), December.

Baden-Powell, B. H. 1974 [1892]. *Land Systems of British India: A Manual of Land Tenure and Systems of Administration Prevalent in Several Provinces*, 3 vols. Oxford: Clarendon Press.

Barnett, David. 2000. 'Is Water Necessarily Identical to H2O?' *Philosophical Studies* 98 (1), 99–112.

Barsh, Russel Lawrence. 1986. 'Indigenous Peoples: An Emerging Object of International Law'. *American Journal of International Law* 80 (2), 369–385.

——. 1987. 'Revision of ILO Convention No. 107'. *The American Journal of International Law* 81 (3), July.

Bate, Marston. 1952. *Where Winter Never Comes: A Study of Man and Nature in the Tropics*. New York: Charles Scribner & Sons.

Beck, David, and Yvonne Lam. n.d. 'Language Loss and Linguistic Suicide: A Case Study from Sierra Norte de Puebla, Mexico'. Toronto Working Papers in Linguistics, 27. Available at https://sites.ualberta.ca/~dbeck/Chambers.pdf (accessed June 2023).

Belmekki, Belkacem. 2008. 'A Wind of Change: The New British Colonial Policy in Post-revolt India'. *Atlantis—Journal of Spanish Association of Anglo-American Studies* 30 (2).

Berat, Lynn. 1993. 'Genocide: The Namibian Case against Germany'. *Pace International Law Review* 5 (1), 165–210.

Bhatia, Bela. 2005. 'Competing Concerns: Commentary'. *Economic and Political Weekly* 40 (47), 19 November.

Bortoft, Henri. 1996. *The Wholeness of Nature: Goethe's Way of Science*. UK: Floris Books.

Bose, Indranil. 2010. 'How Did the Indian Forest Rights Act 2006, Emerge?' IPPG Discussion Paper Series No. 39, University of Manchester. Available at www.ippg.org.uk (accessed May 2023).

Bourdieu, Pierre, Jean-Claude Chamboredon, and Jean-Claude Passeron. 1991. *The Craft of Sociology: Epistemological Preliminaries*, Beate Krais (ed.), and Richard Nice (trans.). Berlin, New York: Walter de Gruyter.

Briggs, John. 2005. 'The Use of Indigenous Knowledge in Development: Problems and Challenges'. *Progress in Development Studies* 5 (2).

Butler, Rhett A. 2005. 'How did Rainforest Shamans Gain their Boundless Knowledge on Medicinal Plants?' *Mongabay*, 14 May. Available at http://news.mongabay.com/2005/0515-rhett_butler.html (accessed May 2023).

Butler, Tina. 2005. 'Shamans and Robots: Bridging the Past and Future of Ethnobotany and Bioprospecting'. *Mongabay*, 25 April. Available at https://news.mongabay.com/2005/04/shamans-and-robots-bridging-the-past-and-future-of-ethnobotany-and-bioprospecting/ (accessed May 2023).

Chakravarty, Anupam. 2016. 'Baigas Get Home'. *DownToEarth*, 15 February. Available at https://www.downtoearth.org.in/news/governance/baigas-get-home-52666 (accessed June 2023).

Chang, Hasok. 2012. *Is Water H2O? Evidence, Realism and Pluralism*. Heidelberg, London, and New York: Springer.

Chatterjee, Partha (ed.). 2013 [2010]. *The Small Voice of History—Ranajit Guha*. New Delhi: Permanent Black.

Chatterjee, Suniti Kumar. 1971. '"Adivasi" Literature of India: Uncultivated "Adivasi" Languages'. *Indian Literature* 14 (3), September.

Choubey, K. N. 2013. 'Do "Pragatisheel" Kanoonon ki Dastan: Rajya, Jan-andolan aur Pratirodh'. *Pratiman: Samay Samaj Sankriti* 1 (1), 149–177.

Clarke, Gerard. 2001. 'From Ethnocide to Ethnodevelopment? Ethnic Minorities and Indigenous Peoples in Southeast Asia'. *Third World Quarterly* 22 (3), 413–436.

Claus, Martina, and Sebastian Hartig. 2018. 'The Koel Karo Hydel Project: An Empirical Study of the Resistance Movement of the Adivasi in Jharkhand/India'. University of Kassel, Germany. Available at chrome-extension://efaidnbmnnnibpcajpcglclefindmkaj/https://www.adivasi-koordination.de/wpdev/wp-content/uploads/2018/02/diplomarbeit-koel-karo-summary.pdf (accessed June 2023).

Clech Lam, Maivan. 2004. 'Remembering the Country of their Birth: Indigenous Peoples and Territoriality'. *Journal of International Affairs* 57 (2).

Cox, Paul, and Michel J. Balick. 1994. 'The Ethnobotanical Approach to Drug Discovery'. *Scientific American* 270 (6), 82–87. Available at https://files.wri.org/d8/s3fs-public/pdf/worldresources1992-93_bw.pdf (accessed August 2023).

Crowley, Timothy J. 2005. 'On the Use of Stoicheion in the Sense of "Element"'. *Oxford Studies in Ancient Philosophy* 29.

de Gila-Kochanowski, Vania. 1983. 'Extracts from the Study: Causes and Consequences of Nomadism among the Gypsies of Europe'. UNESCO Meeting of Experts on the Study of Ethno-development and Ethnocide. Karasjok, Norway, 29 May–2 June.

Devdutt. 2002. *WTO: A Challenge for Swadeshi Swaraj*. New Delhi: Pragya Sansthan.

Diamond, Jared. 2008. 'What's your consumption factor?' *Pacific Ecologist* 16 (Winter).

Eraker, Harald. 2000. 'CO2lonialism—Norwegian Tree Plantations, Carbon Credits and Land Conflicts in Uganda'. Norwatch, Norway.

Foster, John Bellamy. 2000. *Marx's Ecology: Materialism and Nature*. New York: Monthly Review Press.

Fricker, Miranda. 2007. *Epistemic Injustice: Power and the Ethics of Knowing*. Oxford: Oxford University Press.

Fukuoka, Masanobu. 2001 [1978]. *The One-Straw Revolution: An Introduction to Natural Farming*. Mapusa, Goa: The Other India Press.

Gandhi, Ramchandra. 2005. 'A Great Forest Debate'. In Savyasaachi (ed.), *Between the Earth and the Sky*. New Delhi: Penguin India.

Ghosal, Somnath. 2011. 'Pre-Colonial and Colonial Forest Culture in the Presidency of Bengal'. *Human Geographies: Journal of Studies and Research in Human Geography* 5 (1).

Ghosh, Padmaparna. 2007. 'Tribals say they are being denied self-governance, move court'. *Mint*, 5 November. Available at https://www.livemint.com/Politics/k5HnaYhDGQccaR6WnvVFAJ/Tribals-say-they-are-being-denied-selfgovernance-move-cour.html (accessed June 2023).

Glenn, Lori. 2005. 'Ethnobotany: An Adventure into the Origin of Herbal Medicine'. *HerbClip News*, published by the American Botanical Council, 15 August. Available at http://herbalgram.org/resources/herbclip/herbclip-news/2005/ethnobotany-an-adventure-into-the-origin-of-herbal-medicine/ (accessed May 2023).

Government of India. 2013. *Statistical Profile of Scheduled Tribes in India*. Noida: Ministry of Tribal Affairs, Statistical Division; Chaar Dishayen Printers.

Government of India. 2014. *Report of the High Level Committee on Socio-Economic, Health and Educational Status of Tribal Communities of India*. New Delhi: Ministry of Tribal Affairs, Government of India.

Grierson, George Abraham. 2001. 'Trinity Monday Discourse', 14 May. Available at https://www.tcd.ie/Secretary/FellowsScholars/discourses/discourses/2001_S%20Sen%20on%20A%20Grierson.pdf (accessed June 2023).

Grigson, W. V. 1944. 'The Aboriginal in the Future'. *The Journal of the Royal Anthropological Institute of Great Britain and Ireland* 74 (½).

Grove, Richard. 1995. *Green Imperialism: Colonial Expansion, Tropical Island Edens and the Origins of Environmentalism, 1600–1800*. Cambridge: Cambridge University Press.

Guha, Ramachandra. 1996. 'Savaging the Civilised: Verrier Elwin and the Tribal Question in Late Colonial Times'. *Economic and Political Weekly* 31 (35/37), 2375–2389.

Guha, Ranajit. 1983. *Elementary Aspects of Peasant Insurgency in Colonial India*. Delhi: Oxford University Press.

Gulli, Bruno. 2005. *Labor of Fire: The Ontology of Labor between Economy and Culture*. Philadelphia: Temple University Press.

Hebbar, Ritambhara. 2011. *Ecology, Equality and Freedom: The Engagement with Self-Rule in Jharkhand*. Navi Mumbai: Earthworm Books.

Hirtz, Frank. 2003. 'It Takes Modern Means to be Traditional: On Recognizing Indigenous Cultural Communities in the Philippines'. *Development and Change* 34 (5), 887–914.

Hulswit, Menno. 1996. 'Teleology: A Peircean Critique of Ernst Mayr's Theory', *Transactions of the Charles S. Peirce Society* 32 (2), 188–191.

Ilyenkov, E. V. 2013 [1960]. *Dialectics of the Abstract and the Concrete in Marx's Capital*, Sergei Syrovatkin (trans.). New Delhi: Aakar Books.

Irigaray, Luce. 1999. *The Forgetting of Air in Martin Heidegger*, Mary Beth Mader (trans.). Austin: University of Texas Press.

Kaiser, Ejaz. 2013. 'Maoist Dances around Cong Leader's Body'. *Hindustan Times*, Indore, 27 May.

Kapila, Kriti. 2008. 'The Measure of a Tribe: The Cultural Politics of Constitutional Reclassification in North India'. *Journal of the Royal Anthropological Institute* (n.s.) 14, 117–134.

Khan, S. A., and H. bin Talal. 1987. *Indigenous Peoples: A Global Quest for Justice*. A Report of the Independent Commission on International Humanitarian Issues (RICIHI). London: Zed Books.

Khosravi Lile, Hadi. 2006. 'A New Era for Indigenous Peoples: The United Nations Permanent Forum on Indigenous Issues'. *Galdu Cala—Journal of Indigenous Rights* 2, 24–25.

Kingsbury, Benedict. 1998. '"Indigenous Peoples" in International Law: A Constructivist Approach to the Asian Controversy'. *The American Journal of International Law* 92 (3), 414–457. Available at https://www.jstor.org/stable/pdf/2997916.pdf (accessed August 2023).

Kishwan, Jagdish, Rajiv Pandey, and V. K. Dadhwal. 2009. 'India's Forest and Tree Cover: Contribution as a Carbon Sink'. Technical Paper, Indian Council of Forestry Research and Education, Dehradun. Available at chrome-extension://efaidnbmnnnibpcajpcglclefindmkaj/https://www.forests.tn.gov.in/tnforest/app/webroot/img/document/gov-india-publication/3.pdf (accessed May 2023).

Knowlton, Edgar C. 1920. 'The Goddess Nature in Early Periods'. *The Journal of English and Germanic Philology* 19 (2), April. Available at https://www.jstor.org/stable/pdf/27701000.pdf?refreqid=excelsior%3A0a9cb1b6c8382c50839a72b4ed967bc1&ab_segments=&origin=&initiator=&acceptTC=1 (accessed August 2023).

Kripke, S. 1980 [1972]. *Naming and Necessity*. Cambridge: Harvard University Press.

Kumar, Sanjay. 2001. 'Indigenous Communities' Knowledge of Local Ecological Services'. *Economic and Political Weekly* 36 (30), 28 July.

Kumar, V. Sraavya Rajasri. 2019. 'Gondi Language: Identity, Politics and Struggle in India'. *IQSR Journal of Humanities and Social Sciences (IQSR-JHSS)* 24 (2), Series 7 (February).

Leonard, William E. 1908. *The Fragments of Empedocles*. London: The Open Court Publishing Company.

Levi-Strauss, Claude. 1966 [1962]. *The Savage Mind* (*La Pensee Sauvage*), George Weindenfeld (trans.). Illinois, Chicago: University of Chicago Press. Available at https://www.scribd.com/document/425653251/The-Savage-Mind-pdf# (accessed August 2023).

——. 1985. *The View from Afar*, Joachim Neugroschel and Phoebe Hoss (trans.), esp. Chapter 13, 186-187. New York: Basic Books.

Lukacs, Georg. 1980 [1978]. *The Ontology of Social Being: 3. Labour*, David Fernbach (trans.). London: Merlin Press. Available at https://www.marxists.org/archive/lukacs/works/ontology/ontology-social-being-vol3.pdf (accessed August 2023).

Luxemburg, Rosa. 1951. *Accumulation of Capital*, Agnes Schwarzschild (trans.), with a new Introduction by Tadeusz Kowalik. London, New York: Routledge & Kegan Paul.

Madhu, Aparna. 2017. 'PESA: A Mere Mirage of Independent Local Self-Governance'. *NUJS Journal of Regulatory Studies* 2 (1), 82–91. Available at chrome-extension://efaidnbmnnnibpcajpcglclefindmkaj/https://

www.nujs.edu/wp-content/uploads/2022/11/File-38.pdf (accessed May 2023).

Mander, Jerry, and Victoria Tauli-Corpuz (eds). 2006. *Paradigm Wars: Indigenous People's Resistance to Globalization*. San Francisco: Sierra Club Books.

Merchant, Carolyn. 1980. *The Death of Nature: Women, Ecology and the Scientific Revolution*. USA: Harper and Row.

Miller, David Philip. 2004. *Discovering Water: James Watt, Henry Cavendish and the Nineteenth-Century 'Water Controversy'*, Science, Technology and Culture, 1700–1945. New York: Routledge.

Ministry of Environment, Forest and Climate Change. 2019. 'Centre releases Rs. 47,436 crores for afforestation to various states'. PIB Delhi, 29 August. Available at https://pib.gov.in/PressReleaseIframePage.aspx?PRID=1583452 (accessed June 2023).

Mitchell, Juliet. 1998. 'Trauma, Recognition, and the Place of Language'. *Diacritics* 28 (4), Winter.

Mohd. Ali Faraz, Rajanya Bose, Sajjad Hassan, and Sandeep Ghusale. 2016. *The Extent and Nature of Individual Tribal Land Alienation in the Fifth Schedule States in India: A Study*. New Delhi: Centre for Equity Studies. Available at https://archive.nyu.edu/bitstream/2451/42252/2/Extent%20and%20Nature%20of%20Individual%20Tribal%20Land%20Alienation.pdf (accessed June 2023).

Moody, R. (ed.). 1988. *Indigenous Voices: Visions and Realities*, 2 vols. London: Zed Books.

Munda, R. D., and Sanjay Bosu Mullick (eds). 2003. *The Jharkhand Movement: Indigenous People's Struggle for Autonomy in India*. Copenhagen: International Work Group for Indigenous Affairs. Available at Available at: https://www.iwgia.org/images/publications/0120_jharkhand_movement.pdf (accessed August 2023).

Narayanan, Dinesh. 2015. 'Forest Rights Act: How Rules Fail in the Jungle'. *The Economic Times*, 1 October. Available at https://m.economictimes.com/news/economy/policy/forest-rights-act-how-rules-fail-in-the-jungle/articleshow/49175798.cms (accessed March 2023).

Nayar, Baldev Raj. 1998. 'Political Structure and India's Economic Reforms of the 1990s'. *Pacific Affairs* 71 (3), 335–358.

Nozaki, Yukiko. 2023. 'Rise of Carbon Farming in India: World's Largest Agrarian Country Expected to Become the Leading Market for Carbon Farming Credits'. Mitsui and Co. Global Strategic Studies Institute Monthly Report, February. Available at https://www.mitsui.com/mgssi/en/report/detail/__icsFiles/afieldfile/2023/03/28/2302i_nozaki_e.pdf (accessed June 2023).

Padel, Felix, and Samrendra Das. 2006. 'Anthropology of a Genocide: Tribal Movements in Central India against Over-Industrialisation'. Report for the South Asia Analysis Group (SAAG). Available at http://sanhati.com/wp-content/uploads/2008/08/felixpadel-samarendradas.pdf (accessed May 2023).

Pasayat, Chitrasen. 2008. 'Language and Identity with Special Reference to the Tribal People'. *Orissa Review*, April.

Perelman, Michael. 2007. 'Primitive Accumulation from Feudal Times to Neoliberalism'. *Capitalism, Nature, Socialism* 18 (2).

Planning Commission. 2006. *Report of the Working Group on Land Relations for Formulation of the 11th Five-Year Plan*. New Delhi: Government of India.

Poffenberger, Mark, Emmanuel O'Shea, et al. 2002. 'The Clean Development Mechanism and Village-Based Forest Restoration: A Case Study from Adilabad District, Andhra Pradesh, India'. Report, Community Forestry International. Available at https://www.academia.edu/25487473/The_clean_development_mechanism_and_village_based_forest_restoration (accessed May 2023).

Popke, E. Jeffery. 2003. 'Managing Colonial Alterity: Narratives of Race Space and Labor in Durban, 1870–1920'. *Journal of Historical Geography* 29 (2), 248–267.

Poupart, Lisa M. 2003. 'The Familiar Face of Genocide: Internalized Oppression among American Indians'. *Hypatia* 18 (2).

Prasad, Archana. 2003. *Against Ecological Romanticism: Verrier Elwin and the Making of an Anti-Modern Tribal Identity*. New Delhi: Three Essays Collective.

Ramnath, M. 1988. 'Predicting the Monsoon: Modern Science vs. Traditional Wisdom'. *The Ecologist* 18 (6).

Rani, Midatala. 2000. 'Tribal Languages and Tribal Education'. *Social Action* 50 (4), October–December, 414–419.

Roy Burman, B. K. 1998. 'Workers Depend on Forest Ecology for Subsistence: Their Problems and Prospects'. Keynote Address, presented at the workshop on 'Status of Forest Workers in India', Chandigarh, 29 April.

Saeed, Saima. Forthcoming. *Media's Romance of the 'Reds': Myth-Making, the Maoist Insurgency and the News 'Text'*.

Sandars, N. K. 1972 [1960]. *The Epic of Gilgamesh*, English version. London: Penguin Classics.

Sanyal, Kaushiki. 2006. 'STs (Recognition of Forest Rights) Bill'. *India Together*, 15 April. Available at http://www.indiatogether.org/2006/apr/law-forest.htm (accessed May 2023).

Sartre, Jean Paul. 2004. *Critique of Dialectical Reason*, Vol 1. Jonathan Ree (ed.), Alan Sheridan-Smith (trans.), and with a Foreword by Fredric Jameson. London: Verso.

Savyasaachi. 2004. 'Indigenous Peoples and Their Life Support Systems: A Perspective on Production Processes'. In Eleonora Barbieri-Masini (ed.), *Quality of Human Resources: Disadvantaged People*, in *Encyclopedia of Life Support Systems (EOLSS)*, developed under the auspices of the UNESCO. Oxford, UK; Eolss Publishers. Available at http://www.eolss.net (accessed May 2023).

—— (ed.). 2005. *Between the Earth and the Sky: The Penguin Book of Forest Writings*. New Delhi: Penguin Books.

Sengupta, Papia. 2009. 'Endangered Languages: Some Concerns'. *Economic and Political Weekly* 44 (32), 8 August, 17–19.

Seth, D. L. 2014. 'Globalization and the New Politics of Micro-Movements'. In Savyasaachi and Ravi Kumar (eds), *Social Movements: Transformative Shifts and Turning Points*. New Delhi: Routledge.

Shah, Mihir. 2005. 'First You Push Them in and Then You Throw Them out'. *Economic and Political Weekly* 40 (47), 19–25 November, 4895–4899.

Simpson, Smith. 1939. 'Twenty-fifth Session of the International Labor Conference'. *The American Journal of International Law* 33 (4), 716–725. Available at https://www.jstor.org/stable/2192882 (accessed May 2023).

Social Watch. 2004. 'Fear and Want—Obstacles to Human Security'. Available at https://www.socialwatch.org/annualReport/2004 (accessed May 2023).

Sperber, Dan, Fabrice Clement, Christophe Heintz, Olivier Mascaro, Hugo Mercier, Gloria Origgi, and Deirdre Wilson. 2010. 'Epistemic Vigilance'. *Mind & Language* 25 (4), September.

Springate-Baginski, O., M. Sarin, S. Ghosh, P. Dasgupta, I. Bose, A. Banerjee, K. Sarap, P. Misra, S. Behera, M. G. Reddy, and P. T. Rao. 2009. 'Redressing "Historical Injustice" through the Indian Forest Rights Act 2006: A Historical Institutional Analysis of Contemporary Forest Rights Reform'. IPPG Discussion Paper Series No. 27, University of Manchester. Available at www.ippg.org.uk (accessed May 2023).

Srivastava, Vinay Kumar. 2010. 'Religion and Development, India'. Working Paper Series, 1 (3). New Delhi: Indian Institute of Dalit Studies and Religions and Development Research Program.

Stauffer, Jill. 2015. *Ethical Loneliness: The Injustice of Not Being Heard*. New York: Columbia University Press.

Stocking, Jr., George W. (ed.). 1983. *Observers Observed: Essays on Ethnographic Fieldwork*. London: The University of Wisconsin Press. Available at https://letrasindomitas.files.wordpress.com/2018/03/observers-observed-essays-on-e-george-w-stocking-jr.pdf (accessed August 2023).

Sundar, Nandini. 2005. 'Custom and Democracy in Jharkhand'. *Economic and Political Weekly* 40 (41), 8–14 October, 4430–4434.

Supreme Court of India. 2011. *Civil Original Jurisdiction, Writ petition (Civil)* No. 180.

Swepston, Lee. 1989. 'Indigenous and Tribal Peoples and International Law: Recent Developments'. *Current Anthropology* 30 (2), 259–264.

Sztompka, Piotr. 2000. 'The Ambivalence of Social Change Triumph or Trauma?' *Polish Sociological Review* 131.

Uberoi, J. P. S. 1984. *The Other Mind of Europe: Goethe as a Scientist*. New Delhi: Oxford University Press.

——. 2002. *European Modernity: Science, Truth and Method*. New Delhi: Oxford University Press.

Uberoi, J. P. S., and Khalid Tyabji (ed.). 2019. *Mind and Society: From Indian Studies to General Sociology*. New Delhi: Oxford University Press.

UNESCO. 1981. 'UNESCO and the Struggle against Ethnocide: Declaration of San Jose', December. USA: San Jose. Available at https://unesdoc.unesco.org/ark:/48223/pf0000049951 (accessed May 2023).

Upadhyay, S. 2004. 'Tribal Self-rule Law and Common Property Resources in Scheduled Areas of India: A New Paradigm Shift or Another Ineffective Sop?' Paper presented at 'The Commons in an Age of Global Transition: Challenges, Risks and Opportunities', 10th Biennial Conference of IASCP, organised by the International Association for the Study of Common Property at Oaxaca, Mexico, 9–13 August.

Veilleux, Connie, Steven R. King, and Linda Morganstein. n.d. 'An Introduction to Ethnobotany'. Available at http://www.entheology.org/shaman-ethnobotany/ethnobotany.htm (accessed May 2023).

Verso, Eric. 2015. 'Topsoil Erosion'. Submitted to Stanford University, 9 December. Available at http://large.stanford.edu/courses/2015/ph240/verso2/ (accessed June 2023).

von Werlhof, Claudia. 2000. '"Globalization" and "Permanent" Processes of "Primitive Accumulation": The Example of the MAI, and Multilateral Agreement on Investment'. *Journal of World-Systems Research*, Special Issue: Festchrift for Immanuel Wallerstein—Part II, VI (3).

Ward, Tony. 2009. 'Antiquity, Forest and Simmel's Sociology of Value'. Available at https://www.researchgate.net/publication/228223926_Antiquities_Forests_and_Simmel's_Sociology_of_Value (accessed May 2023).

Wright, Robin M. 1988. 'Anthropological Presuppositions of Indigenous Advocacy'. *Annual Review of Anthropology* 17 (1), 365–390.

World Commission on Environment and Development (WCED). 1987. *Our Common Future*. Delhi: Oxford University Press.

World Resources. 1992–1993. *A Guide to the Global Environment: A Report by the World Resource Institute.* New York: Oxford University Press. Available at https://files.wri.org/d8/s3fs-public/pdf/worldresources1992-93_bw.pdf (accessed August 2023).

Yupsanis, Athanasios. 2010. 'ILO Convention No 169 Concerning Indigenous and Tribal Peoples in Independent Countries, 1989–2009: An Overview'. *Nordic Journal of International Law* 79, 433–456.

Index